THE "CHINESE" WAY OF DOING THINGS:

Perspectives on American-Born Chinese and
the Chinese Church in North America

Samuel Ling
with Clarence Cheuk

CHINA HORIZON

P.O. Box 2209, San Gabriel, CA 91778

HORIZON MINISTRIES CANADA

201-745 Broadway, Vancouver, BC V5Z 4J7

Distributed by

P U B L I S H I N G
P.O.BOX 817 • PHILLIPSBURG • NEW JERSEY 08865-0817

HORIZON SERIES
Samuel Ling, General Editor

The "Chinese Way" of Doing Things:
Perspectives on American-Born Chinese
and the Chinese Church in North America

Samuel Ling
with Clarence Cheuk

China Horizon, San Gabriel 91778
Horizon Ministries Canada, Vancouver
© 1999 by China Horizon and Horizon Ministries Canada
All rights reserved. Published 1999.
ISBN 1-892-63202-0

7. 66 ×

101535

CONTENTS

Acknowledgments

Although I am solely responsible for the content of this book, I am indebted to many people who have participated, encouraged, and contributed during the editing process.

Dr. Tony Carnes and Rev. Alex Yeung are two among my friends who have constantly encouraged me to write and publish. The Lord has used them and others to push me on. During the conceptualization stage of this book, Mrs. Felicity Bentley-Taylor of Great Britain offered invaluable critical remarks, giving initial shape to the book. Dr. Hoover Wong, Senior Professor at Fuller School of World Mission, offered very helpful critiques. Clarence Cheuk, a student in my Asian History class at Wheaton College, spent an entire summer interviewing his fellow Asian Americans; the result, plus his own understanding of Generation X, form the content of chapters one and two. My colleagues at the Institute for Chinese Studies at Wheaton College, and my colleagues Janet Chen, Teresa Chia and Arthur Hsu in Pasadena, California, spent many hours editing, proofreading and formatting this manuscript.

Mr. William Tsui of Christian Communications Inc. of Canada has been supportive of our writing and publishing efforts through the years. Rev. Sam Chan and Rev. Alex Yeung were kind enough to offer written responses to chapter two, from the perspective of the Chinese church.

I would like to thank the editors of the following publications for granting permission to reprint part or all of the following chapters in this volume:

Chapter 3 appeared as "Facing the Crisis in Our Time," *Chinese Around the World*, July 1997: Chinese Coordination Centre of World Evangelism, Hong Kong.

Chapters 4, 5, 6, 7 and 13, "Chinese-ness And Ourselves: Resolving the Perplexities of Locating the Chinese Community in North America," *CGST Journal*, No. 19 (July 1995): China Graduate School of Theology, Hong Kong.

Chapter 8, "The 'Chinese' Way of Doing Things: Contours of OBC-ABC Cultural Differences," from *Chinese Around the World*, June 1984, July 1984, and August 1984.

Chapter 9, "A Bicultural Profile of Chinese Churches in North America," from *Chinese Churches in North America*, January-February 1990: Chinese Coordination Centre of World Evangelism — North America (CCCOWE-NA).

Chapter 10 appeared as "Ten Trends of Urban Ministry For the Chinese Church," *Challenger*, January 1993 and February 1993, Chinese Christian Mission, Petaluma, California.

Chapter 11, "Beyond the 'Chinese' Way of Doing Things: Cultural Diversity, Cultural Change and the Continued Search for a Theology of Culture," *Chinese Around the World*, March 1985, and April 1985: Chinese Coordination Centre of World Evangelism.

Chapter 12, "Bridging Racial and Linguistic Gaps" was originally presented at the Ethnic Chinese Congress on World Evangelization, Honolulu, July 1984.

The Afterword appeared in abbreviated form as "People as Onions," *Challenger*: April 1987, Chinese Christian Mission, Petaluma, California.

Finally, I am indebted to the many readers who first read the chapters of this book on the pages of periodicals such as *Chinese Around the World, Challenger,* and *China Graduate School of Theology Journal*. They have offered their encouragement and suggestions, often during my visit to their churches and regional conferences. I would like to thank the editors of these and other magazines who have encouraged and challenged me to write in response to burning issues in the Chinese church. Some of the most helpful critical suggestions have come from Asian Americans of the 1990s. They have opened my eyes to the increasingly complex picture of the cultural milieu within which the twenty-first century Chinese church lives, moves and has her being. It is to them, and for the Body of Christ at large, that this volume is dedicated. My prayer is that the people of God may be encouraged and challenged.

To God be all the glory.

Samuel Ling

Introduction

What Time Is It?

Anyone who wants to do God's will and make a difference in the world today must ask a critical question: What time is it? At what point in history has God called me to serve him?

What time is it in your life right now? What are you doing? Are you having your morning coffee break? Are you having lunch? Is it sunrise or sunset? According to Psalm 90, if you are in your thirties, chances are that more than half of your life is behind you by now. How will you invest the rest of your life?

A Quest for Churchhood

What time is it in the Chinese church? The history of the Chinese church has been a story of beginnings, a story of "starting over again." Robert Morrison came to China in 1807; but, after nearly a century of pioneering and expanding missionary work, the Boxer Uprising in 1900 brought China to her knees before the West. The Chinese church "started all over again," this time rebuilding on the blood of martyrs. In 1927, after five years of the Anti-Christian Movement, five thousand of the eight thousand Protestant missionaries in China went back home, never to return to China again. Chinese Christians, awakened to their responsibility to build an indigenous Chinese church, "began all over again." In 1937, as Japan invaded mainland China, many of the Nationalist forces migrated to western China, and many Chinese Christians went along. The Chinese church was built in Sichuan and other inland provinces through revivals among students. In 1949, after the Communist Revolution, the churches in China, as well as Chinese churches overseas (notably in Taiwan and Hong Kong), started all over again as "the church in exile," or a "refugee church." Then in the 1960s, with the influx of Chinese students coming to North America, the new Chinese church began to be built as well.

What about the twenty-first century? Are we ready to move on beyond the "starting over again" phase, to build something more mature and more permanent, something which bears a meaningful relationship to our social context (global culture) and to history? Yes, we have moved from evangelism, to discipleship, to building church buildings and calling pastors; we are even moving toward missions (at least many churches have a missions budget and participate in short-term mission projects). But, are we ready for a more mature, more permanent and full-fledged "churchhood" status? Indeed, what time is it in the Chinese church in North America?

Sunset Over Three Empires

What time is it in China? A theologian from Singapore witnessed the June 1989 Tiananmen Square event with his very own eyes. He painted two word pictures of the incident at a subsequent missions convention. In the first image it was dusk, and from his hotel window he looked down at Chang An Avenue. Thousands of Beijing citizens were going home after a day's work, either on foot or on bicycles. They were all walking towards a red, setting sun. The "red sun" was setting in China.

The second picture portrayed morning in Inner Mongolia. As the speaker took a walk on the plains, he saw a fluttering white on the horizon. He could not tell what it was until it moved closer to him. Then he saw it: they were sheep. But more than that, he saw a shepherd, and the shepherd was carrying a staff.

A red sun setting... The shepherd and his sheep approaching on the horizon... Is this what time it is in China? Is this what time it is among the Chinese people? If we extend this analogy further, we can see that we are truly living in a moment in history with global consequences. Chinese civilization has repeatedly come to a dead end in the twentieth century. To borrow an image from the film, *The Last Emperor*, the Chinese people kept coming to a closed door or a closed gate. The 1911 revolution brought an end to the imperial dynasty, while 1949 brought an end to Nationalist rule on the mainland. But every time there was change, there was no change as well. The democracy movement in 1989 seemed to spell an end to a kind of closed-door mentality. But where is the open door? And where does the door open to?

Eastern Europe, with the tremendous changes taking place in the fall of 1989, had come to an end of an era. What kind of model will now emerge? Would it be a model of selfish individualism, or a model of freedom with order, purpose, and discipline? In fact, in certain parts of Eastern Europe today, we find leaders and people with determination to instill an ethical purpose into their nation's destiny.

If we look at the United States, we can see that she, too, has come to an end of an era. Yale historian, Sydney Ahlstrom, commented at the end of his book, *A Religious History of the American People*, that while the Renaissance and the Reformation of the sixteenth century marked the beginning of the modern,

Christian West, the assassination of John F. Kennedy in 1963 spelled the end of the Christian era. *Time* magazine devoted an issue in 1987 to "leadership." The editors wrote, "The nation looked for leaders, and no one was home." Has America come to an end of an era as well? Is the United States no longer "Number One"? Has the Manifest Destiny been bestowed on some other people?

What will the twenty-first century bring? We do not have in mind whether nations such as Japan, or a united Germany, or even China, will dominate the global economy or the geopolitical scene. Our concern is this: the world is getting smaller and smaller each day. A global culture is emerging. Wherever one travels in the world, one is confronted by the urban phenomenon where cities are total systems, where people are always on the move (migration), and where the rich get richer and the poor get poorer. No matter which nation one travels to, the airports all look the same, the hotels all look the same, and the gift shops and restaurants all accept Visa and American Express. We truly live in a global culture dominated and influenced by the secular materialism coming out of the "cultural wombs" of New York, Los Angeles, London, Paris, and Hong Kong. But with the falling out of three global empires — the Chinese, Russian, and American — who will now guide the emerging global culture? What will be at the core of the culture of the twenty-first century? Would it be raw, selfish materialism? Or will the gospel of Jesus Christ take its rightful place at the heart of the new cultural synthesis that is now emerging? That is the question. And that is why it is so important to know: what time is it?

Are We Ready for Tomorrow's ABC Ministries?

What time is it in Chinese America? What time is it in Chinese American ministries?

In 1976 I began ministry among American-born Chinese young people in a Chinatown church in New York City. At that time few churches were looking for ABC youth workers. Instead, the young people sought outside speakers (mostly overseas-born Chinese, or OBCs) for spiritual nourishment, while pastors and church leaders, mostly recent immigrants, repeated the often-heard slogan — "You are Chinese — we are a Chinese church — you should speak Chinese!" In the 1970s, the challenge was evangelism, discipleship, and incorporating American-born Chinese (ABCs) into an OBC-dominated church scene.

That OBC-centered slogan is seldom heard today as the twenty-first century dawns upon us. I often get phone calls requesting for a part-time ABC youth worker, or sometimes a church would request a full-time English pastor. I also receive frequent requests for advice on starting an English worship service. Churches are asking: Is this the right time? Will it split the church?

Things are different in the 1990s. The proportion of ABCs in the Chinese community has not increased; in fact, it has decreased a little due to the waves of immigration coming from mainland China, Indochina, as well as the traditional places (Taiwan, Hong Kong and Southeast Asia) in the past twenty years. But, the absolute number of ABCs has increased. The difference in today's climate, so much more favorable to ABC ministries, is due to the awakening of OBC leadership. Simply put, they now recognize the needs of ABC people.

There are over eight hundred Chinese churches in North America today. The vast majority of them were either started in the last twenty-five years, and/or are now led by OBC professionals who, twenty-five years ago, were visa students in a foreign land. Twenty-five years ago most of the churches in

Chinatown had a long history, and the young people in them were children of Toisan immigrants from the early days (whom I call "classic ABCs"). But, not so today. Churches led by OBC professionals are now located both in Chinatowns and in suburbia or outlying areas such as: Monterey Park, Diamond Bar, and Irvine in Southern California; Scarborough and Richmond Hill in Ontario; and Flushing and Long Island in New York. What is important to note here is that the children of the pastors and church board members have now reached college age. This new generation of ABCs are children of professionals; they are more outgoing, achievement- and competition-oriented, better dressed, and are more inclined to enter prestigious universities. Church leaders, not willing to lose this generation of young adults, are crying out for help. They are looking for pastors to lead youth groups and to start English worship services. Pastors are learning ministry strategies and models that cater to ABCs. All have a desire to see the church grow.

Who will be pastoring tomorrow's ABC congregations? My guess is that by the year 2020, there will be at least fifteen hundred Chinese churches. My estimation is that currently there are no more than two hundred English ministries. By "English ministry" I mean an English worship service with a pastoral staff member. I do not mean a children's worship service or some kind of "junior church." (English ministry should be defined just as Chinese ministry is defined — to include worship, education, nurture and fellowship, evangelism service, discipline, and world missions.) We need "parallel ministries."

What about the year 2020? Are we ready?

If we are just to keep up with the present percentage — that is, one English ministry for every four Chinese churches — we will need three hundred seventy-five English ministries. In other words, we are lacking one hundred seventy-five English ministries today. This assumes that the present ABC pastors do not get burned out, discouraged, and leave the Chinese church, and that retired pastors are being replaced.

And when we see the emergence of one hundred seventy-five new English ministries (with pastors) by 2020, we will still be 1,125 English ministries short! Who will be building the ABC ministries in these 1,125 churches? How can we meet this tremendous need? Keep in mind that the immigrant wave today (dominated by mainland Chinese, or PRCs) will simply produce thousands more ABCs tomorrow — ABCs of yet another cultural type. Are we ready for these challenges?

The Goals of Mission

The New Testament spells out for us what it means to make disciples of all nations, baptizing them... and teaching them all that Jesus Christ has commanded us (Matthew 28:19-20). To fulfill the Great Commission of Jesus Christ means to call for the obedience that comes from faith among the nations (Romans 1:5). Certainly this includes the following:

1. *Conversion of men, women, and children.* We witness this happening by the thousands in the first few chapters in the Acts of the Apostles. Among the Chinese population worldwide, only 5% have been Christianized. We have a great task.

2. *Establishment of the church of Jesus Christ* in every major geographical area and culture, with a leadership which is gifted by the Holy Spirit, and therefore capable of expounding the Word of God and applying it to the sheep of Jesus Christ in their cultural settings. We find the

Apostle Paul starting churches and ordaining elders everywhere he went; later he would follow-up on these elder-shepherds, including writing letters to address some of their doctrinal and ethical issues. While people like to talk about the indigenization and contextualization of the church and her theology, it is probably more profitable to speak of the maturation of the church, or the attainment of true "churchhood" as the second goal in the Great Commission. To this end the Chinese church has merely gotten started.

3. Once a church moves beyond the pioneering, evangelistic stage to a growth process towards maturity, she needs to address the vital issues in the society and culture around her. This is the challenge of *transformation of culture*. We find Paul doing this as he addresses the intellectuals in Athens in Acts 17. This is what he has in mind in II Corinthians 10:4-5, when he speaks of defeating the strongholds of secular thought, and holding every thought captive to the obedience of Christ. We find the Apostle John alluding to this as the goal of all things, when in the new heavenly Jerusalem, the princes of the nations will bring their glory (that is, their transformed culture), changed with their living faith in Jesus Christ, into eternity (Revelation 21:24, 26).

True Revival

The church of Jesus Christ needs to pray for revival today. But what is revival? There are two key components to revival, and we find both of these elements present in Ezra's and Nehemiah's time, when the people wept when God's law was read and explained. These two components are also found in some of history's greatest revivals, for example, in the Puritan movement in England and America in the seventeenth century and the Great Awakening in the eighteenth century.

These two key elements are (1) the repentance for sin, and (2) the building and transforming of the Christian mind. Repentance was what the Puritans preached during the Elizabethan era (1558-1603) and during the reign of James I (1603-1620). The Puritans also promoted learning in the Scriptures; this was evident as new colleges such as Emmanuel and Sidney Sussex were started at Cambridge University in 1584 and 1596. The Great Awakening, under the preaching of Theodore Jacobus Frelinghuysen in Raritan, New Jersey (1719-1747), and Jonathan Edwards in Massachusetts (in the 1730s), saw God's people, the visible church, repenting and being converted by the preaching of the gospel. Edwards' famous sermon, "Sinners in the Hands of an Angry God," brought tears to the listeners. George Whitefield preached the same message up and down the thirteen colonies.

These people of God also promoted the training of both a learned and godly ministry, and a learned and godly laity. Gilbert Tennent warned about the "Danger of an Unconverted Ministry," that is, the dangers when ministers are not saved. William Tennent started the Log College in Nashaminey, Pennsylvania, to train a new breed of pastors. The Great Awakening brought about the founding of a great number of colleges, notably Columbia University, Princeton University, Rutgers University, the University of Pennsylvania, and a host of other smaller colleges. The goal was that ministers, as well as lay people, must be trained to think God's thoughts after him. Jonathan Edwards was not only a great preacher, but he was also a great theologian who defended the Christian faith over against the secular Enlightenment of the eighteenth century.

This is what made the Great Awakening great; but, it was this second key element (the building of a Christian mind) that was conspicuously missing in the later revivals of the 1790s and the 1860s-1880s. Dwight Moody's revival called thousands of American and British university students to go overseas to "evangelize this world in our generation," but the gospel brought to China, India, and Africa was often an anti-intellectual and anti-theological gospel. The result was that the Chinese church and Chinese theological education suffered; we have inherited a second-rate model of ministerial training and an anti-culture stance.

It is time for a true revival to take place. It is time to pray and to dig into both the Scriptures (as the base) and a study of the culture around us (as application with transformation as the goal). Where are the Chinese Christians who will pray and think for the Lord?

What message will we bring to our generation? With what kind of gospel will we work towards the transformation of our culture? Will we preach a "full-size" God as he has revealed himself in Scripture, or will we offer a "reduced" deity, someone who is only the God of "spiritual truths" but is incapable of revealing accurate facts when it comes to history and science? Will we preach only vaguely about our "relationship to God" and cater to the psychological needs of people, without specifying the horrible consequences of sin, of an eternity spent without Christ, and of the eternal, heavenly benefits of our salvation? Will we build up the church of Jesus Christ so that she can think with a Christian mind? What message do we have for the Chinese church in America today?

It is time for revival — to pray for it, to work for it, and to build up the Christian mind.

THE "CHINESE" WAY OF DOING THINGS

Setting the Stage

This portion of the book enables you, the reader, to witness the issues, problems, and questions that were raised in the Introduction, "What Time Is It?", by taking a look at the lives of real people. The individuals featured in this section are real-life individuals from real-life Chinese churches. They represent the young Chinese-American Christian condition. Chapter 1, "Our Enigmatic Generation," is an essay written by Clarence Cheuk, when he was a student of philosophy and theology at Wheaton College. He explores in depth the roots of the current Chinese-American mindset. Chapter 2 sketches for you the profiles of ABCX Christians. This is an intimate peek into the minds and hearts of young Chinese-American Christians. They will tell their stories, their frustrations, and their hopes. You may be surprised by their honesty. Uncertainty and despair will show themselves through the thoughts of these Chinese Christians. In this way, we can familiarize ourselves with the questions of the current generation.

Our Enigmatic Generation:
A Second Generation ABCX Perspective

Clarence Cheuk

We are rather enigmatic. So enigmatic that those of us born in America between the mid-'60s and early '80s, have been designated "Generation X." The only thing that this label tells us is that the definition is elusive. We are so messed up that no tidy designation will suffice. The previous generations of the twentieth century have well-defined markings that at least dare to capture the era in some sort of box-like thing. There was the G.I. Generation that was born during the beginning of the century. They were the heroes of World War II who had a great relationship with the United States government. They dominated the White House for thirty-two years, and legislated programs for their own benefit in exchange for an exploding national debt which we, Gen Xers, will have to deal with. Then there was the Silent Generation (born between 1925 and 1942). They emerged during the McCarthy era and submerged quietly into suburbia. They were placid but they were rich, perhaps the richest generation that had ever inhabited the earth. After them came the Baby Boomers (born between 1943 and 1960). After a multitude of wars had spread all over the world, Americans came back home and spread their seeds, creating a massive generation that would eventually go on to define the 1960s and the 1970s.

And out of this rubble comes the most "funky" generation of all, Generation X. Some might say that we are the unlucky, unfortunate ones; we have the privilege of belonging to the thirteenth generation to call ourselves Americans. We have plopped into an environment that challenges our very survival. Many of us are born into broken families, crime-filled neighborhoods, and a society filled with diseases of all sorts (psychological, sexual, and spiritual). We were in debt to our society the instant sperm met egg to form this tattered thing which we only somewhat affectionately refer to as "life." As a result, we are a rather jaded generation that has rejected much of what is fed to us by our elders. The previous generations see us as selfish, materialistic, reckless, non-idealistic, and unpatriotic. We are called "a generation with a PR problem." As the thirteenth generation, we are a curse to our nation and all that it supposedly stands for.

Many say that we are hapless and ill-fated; they blame us for the mindset that we have, as if we alone are responsible for creating ourselves. One Chinese pastor that I spoke to referred to us as "a narcissistic, me-oriented generation that sickens [him]." How nice... True, I believe that we must take some responsibility for our own situation. But, I think that it would be more constructive to see us as a culmination of our past. This, I believe, will allow us to understand the questions of our generation in order to respond with the ultimate answer, Jesus Christ. Sure, it is permissible to essentialize us as a misbehaving generation, but it does not help our understanding and our ministries to simplify something so complex.

For better or for worse, for richer or for poorer, in sickness and in health, we Generation Xers are here, married to the rest of history and about to give birth to the future. We did not magically pop out of some black top hat; we are a "progression" from those generations that went before us. Centuries of Western thought "progression" have worked to create such a bizarre generation. It would serve us all well to work to understand this.

For Christ's sake then, let us learn. Shall we?

In order to understand the modern person, we must understand where we came from. Francis Schaeffer, a Christian theologian and philosopher, traced the history behind modern thought in his book, *Escape From Reason*. He began with Thomas Aquinas, who lived in the thirteenth century. Aquinas' world is divided between the realms of "nature" and "grace." Nature refers to the earthly, tangible, and visible things, while grace refers to God, heaven, souls, and the like. Prior to Aquinas, common thought held that only grace is important; there is no need to delve into "natural" things. However, Aquinas saw no discontinuity between nature and grace. It was his opinion that the Fall in the book of Genesis did not affect the intellect of humankind; it only marred our will. Therefore, humankind's intellect is autonomous. This view opened the way for secular humanism which developed through the Renaissance.

After the Renaissance period (fourteenth to sixteenth century), the Enlightenment (seventeenth and eighteenth century) began to radically transform Western thought. By this time the idea of autonomous intellect was fully developed. Especially after the philosophy of Immanuel Kant, nature has gradually eaten up grace. Nature is rationalistic, logical, deterministic, and unified. Grace is freedom, but it is a kind of freedom which makes no sense. As a result, philosophers like Jacques Rousseau, began to hate science because it was threatening human freedom.

In the nineteenth century, Soren Kierkegaard began to descend what Schaeffer called the "line of despair" in earnest. By this time, the search for a unified field of knowledge for humankind was effectively abandoned. This abandonment was the despair which would be spread down a time line and across to different areas of study, eventually impacting general society and culture. Kierkegaard noted that the natural, rational world is mechanistic and deterministic. There is no hope for humanity in this realm in terms of freedom and optimism. Therefore, humankind must make a leap of faith to the optimistic, but non-rational realm. In other words, there is no rational reason for optimism in this world.

From this philosophy grew twentieth century existentialism. Humankind is dropped into the world with the agonizing freedom to choose or find its own meaning. There are no eternally established guidelines for making choices. There is now a void where meaning once occupied (if it ever even existed, that is). Jean-Paul Sartre filled this void with responsibility, Karl Jaspers with a "final experience," and Timothy Leary with LSD.

This sense of despair has finally spread in our time in the general population. Young people are finding it increasingly difficult, if not impossible, to find any sort of meaning in this mechanical, rational world. The "X" in Generation X is a reminder that the void left by the line of despair has not been filled with anything substantial.

So where are we now? Up until a generation ago, Americans still had some faith in conventional social institutions — politics, the economy, and the family. There was no need for despair since those were intact to a certain degree. Not so any more. One by one, all of those "timeless" social structures are being destroyed before our very eyes.

Politics. Ever since John F. Kennedy's assassination (1963), Richard Nixon and Watergate (1972), and numerous other scandals, very few people in our generation have faith that our political system works for the interests of the people. Also, within the court system, there are different justices for different people. In the 1990s, the Rodney King and the O.J. Simpson cases served only to solidify that mistrust in the system. There is good reason for an entire generation to lose hope in the system.

Economy. One generation ago, and even only one decade ago, Americans could have a great deal of hope for their economic future. But that is not the case today; uncertainty seems to be the consensus concerning our economic security. While an education is becoming increasingly important, educational costs are becoming increasingly overbearing (adjusted average yearly cost of attending a private four-year college in 1970 was $9,000; in 1990, $16,000; in 1997, *Time* magazine published that it cost $31,000 a year to attend the University of Pennsylvania). Whereas Americans of a generation ago could hope to move from engineer to chief engineer, young Americans today have shaky hopes of getting beyond "Do you want fries with that?" Not only are many of us stuck with McJobs trying to pay off McStudentLoans, we will soon be responsible for the national debt and social security (not our own social security, that is). There is good reason to lose faith in the American economic dream.

The family. In the 1960s, the United States experienced what we now call the "Sexual Revolution." We Gen Xers were not there, so I guess we missed out on all the "fun." But we are here to experience the results, and they are definitely not fun. This sexual freedom bound this country to a whole host of social crises — divorce, adultery, unwanted pregnancies, and diseases. As of 1988, only half of all American youths between the ages of fifteen and seventeen lived with both their birth-fathers and birth-mothers. In contrast to the Boomer generation, many Generation

Xers came into the world as unwanted assets. (I am not arguing that non-traditional families cannot be loving, healthy families. I just want to point out the tremendous emotional toll that we, as a nation, are paying as a result of the "Sexual Revolution.") The expectation for a "Leave It To Beaver"-style family is not an expectation at all anymore. There is good reason that our faith in family values is crumbling.

How has the American Christian church ministered to this distraught generation? Apparently not too well. (I realize that I am generalizing, and that generalizations are dangerous and sometimes unfair. I am sure that there are exceptions to the general. However, for the purpose of understanding, I am forced to somewhat generalize.) Take time some day to examine the artistic outlets of Generation X; there is a definite anti-Christian sentiment that saturates them. The collapse of the church as a vehicle of hope in the minds of many Generation Xers is probably the most profound development in the jaded-ness, especially since one of the purposes of the church is to provide hope for a dying world. Besides the church scandals that have surfaced in the last decade and a half (for example, Jim Bakker, Robert Tilton, and cases of sexual abuses by clergy, both Catholic and Protestant), there seems to be something deeper. We must explore....

Modern humanity lives in a void and is in despair, but Americans in previous generations did not have to live with this despair since they had social establishments to put their trust in. For this present generation, these social institutions have collapsed one by one. Therefore, the answer for us Christians should be simple. We can just tell this generation that has lost hope in their world that Jesus Christ is the answer and the hope. What a ripe time for the American Christian church to step in and provide answers, hope, and meaning in life! But we Christians have not done that very well.

What we have often done is reaffirm those values and social enterprises that Generation Xers have already denied, for good reasons, as filling the void. The church tells us that the things we, as a generation, are doing (sex, drugs, suicide, etc.) are empty, and they are correct in saying so. But what the American church is giving us in return as void-fillers are just as empty for us; that is, politics, economy, and family values have no meaning for us. Pat Robertson, the Christian Coalition, Operation Rescue, and the like are all giving the American public the impression that this thing called "Christianity" is an arm of right-wing Republican politics. There is no hope in this for Generation X; we gave that up already. Along with these right-wing values come the advocation of upper-middle-class-ism. The stability of the "good Christian family" can only be achieved with money. Not many today can be so secure about their economic future! The family values that the church promotes are good values, but for many Generation Xers, this is a dead dream.

So the complaints of this generation against the American Christian church are the same complaints it has against the collapsed social enterprises — it provides no satisfaction for the filling of the void, and it is no cure for despair. In other words, it will not save us.

How does this work itself out in the Chinese-American community?

We young Chinese-Americans, as we enter American society either through birth or immigration, have inherited this whole thought pattern. Some have incorporated it within themselves more than others, but all have eaten from the American pie of despair. However, this "line of despair" hits Chinese-America in a unique way. We also have remnants of Confucianism, Taoism, and other "Chinese ways of doing things." We are a complicated swirl of worldviews. Due to historical happenstance, values were wedded within us that possibly were never intended. As a result, we are not understood by our society, by ourselves, and by those who attempt to minister to us. Those who want to minister to us must understand the "chop-suey-ness," the great complexity of the Chinese-American Generation X mind. It is not enough to just tell us to behave, to eat our fried rice, and to like it.

Within such an enigmatic generation, we Chinese-Americans form an even more enigmatic subculture. To make this even more difficult to understand, there is a broad spectrum within the Chinese-American subculture. And to further complicate things, we are constantly on the move within this spectrum. What it comes down to is this: we are more Western than we would like to admit, *and* we are more Chinese than we would like to admit. We young Chinese-Americans are neither Chinese nor American; we are both Chinese *and* American.

In 1995 I moved from lovely San Francisco, conveniently located in the center of my universe at the time, to somewhat-lovely Wheaton, Illinois, to begin my higher education. I should have known that I would be shocked culturally, but I was naive, fresh out of high school. At the time, I thought I could conquer the world and then some. I thought I could handle any changes and ease into any new situation. I was leaving my diverse, urban community in San Francisco for a homogeneously white, suburban community in the middle of Illinois. It has been a rough several years to say the least. There were no Saturday dim sum lunches, no Chinese pastries in those pink boxes with the red string, and no lowered Honda Civics. But worst of all, I was a minority, and I knew it every minute of the day. I felt foreign in my own country of birth. It was then that I realized that I am more Chinese than I ever thought I was before.

In the summer of 1997, I visited Hong Kong for about a week. I was supposed to be at home; this is where my roots are. When I got out of a subway station on my first day there, someone tried to sell me a fake Rolex. Was it that obvious that I was not native? I was seen as foreign in my own ethnic home! I also felt foreign as I walked through the alleyways, searching desperately for any signs of American life. Upon my return to America, I kissed the floor of the San Francisco International Airport; I realized that I was more Western than I ever thought I was.

All of us Chinese-Americans have somehow welded two fundamentally opposed cultures into one. Our Chinese side wills harmony, collectivism, emotional restraint, conformity, and obedience to authority; our Western side opts for individualism, autonomy, and creativity. But as we assimilate more and more into American society, we will inherit more and more of Generation X's worldview. Young Chinese-Americans share in that sense of despair. And it seems as if, like the American churches towards American youth, the Chinese church in America is often giving Chinese-Americans what they have already rejected, for good reasons, as filling the void.

Often the Chinese church in America is preaching Chinese culture in the name of God. It is often done unconsciously, but it is consistently done. There are exhortations to behave in a Chinese way, and not necessarily in a biblical way. However, for many of us (especially young people from non-Christian families), even becoming a Christian is a break with the "Chinese way of doing things," and the Chinese church must realize this. Many church leaders have not realized the complexities of the Chinese-American mind, and as a result, do not understand why the youth act the way that they do. Instead of understanding, they sometimes chastise and call for unquestioned obedience. So the questions of the Western-influenced Chinese-American youth go unnoticed (which is the "proper" way to handle the young people), and therefore, unanswered.

My church life is a good example of this. I grew up in a fairly Americanized home. Cantonese was spoken, though Western values had also infiltrated my family. My parents allowed for our freedom, and in return I offered my respect. I became a Christian during my junior high years. I read the Bible for about three years on my own and decided to accept Christ into my life. I decided to attend church during my freshman year of high school. I attended an Anglo church for a while, but then opted for a large Chinese church in order to meet more young Chinese-American Christians like myself.

Things went well for the first two years at my new Chinese church; I learned to play according to the rules of the game that they set forth. I had gotten my ear pierced the year before I started attending this church. They told me to take my earring off because "Christian guys do not wear earrings." I obeyed unquestioningly at the time... unquestioningly because I was not allowed to question. Questioning was a rebellious act; we were to respect those who were in authority over us by obeying everything that they said. So I obeyed all the rules for the first two years because I wanted to be a good Christian. I served in music ministries, in leadership positions, and in other odd jobs around the church. I learned, over time, my place within the pyramid of power.

But gradually over the next few years, Christianity began to lose meaning for me at that church. It became a bunch of cultural rules that I had to follow in order to save face. On the pulpit the pastor would preach about acceptable hairstyles, music-styles, and of course, that guys should not wear earrings. I knew people in the church who were not very loving, but they were able to abide by the cultural mores. So they were given leadership positions. I also knew the most loving, kindest people who could not operate within the traditional Chinese structure; they were somehow not "spiritual" enough. My Western sense of despair went unnoticed, my questions were acts of rebellion, and my loving friends were objects of disrespect in a church where they did not fit in.

I had to leave the church in order to find something more meaningful. Since moving to Illinois, I have found a Chinese church in Chicago which seems to understand Chinese-Americans. The English pastor preaches from the Bible and not from his cultural beliefs; that is the cure for meaninglessness in life, and that is what stops that dreaded "line of despair." He does not care that I have a hole in my left ear or that I like my hair a certain way. Rather, he is concerned that I am fed from the Word of God. Even the elders at the church seem to care about the young English-speakers. There is something really wonderful about that.

The purpose of this book is understanding — understanding the unique mindset of Chinese-Americans, their questions, and the understanding of ourselves. I realize that I am young and naive (see, there is some Chinese modesty in me!), and I know that I still have a lot to learn about life and about Christianity from those who have gone before me. However, I do believe that the older generation has a lot to learn from us as well.

In the next chapter, you will get a chance to meet several young Chinese-American Christians and you will be able to get a candid peek into their minds and hearts. The issues I have just discussed will come alive in the lives of these believers. You may be shocked, you may even get angry... but please, make an effort to listen, really listen.

Agonies of the Heart:
ABC Christians Speak Out

Edited by
Clarence Cheuk

This is an invitation to you, the reader, to meet the future of the Chinese church in North America. I have collected the thoughts of several young college-aged Chinese-American Christians concerning their cultural identity, Christian growth, and church experiences. I have also included their frustrations with church and hopes for the church. The pieces in this chapter are at times well thought out, and at other times rather raw and emotional. But they are all honest and insightful. Some have found hope and contentment, while others have lost them and found them increasingly elusive. Yet, no matter where on the Chinese-church-contentment spectrum they lie, their Christian faith and their church lives are issues which fill their thoughts. They represent what is going on inside the heads of thousands of young Chinese Christians all over North America. They represent the future leaders and members of the Chinese-American church. For this reason, I believe that we must take their thoughts seriously if we are to minister to the Chinese-American community of the twenty-first century.

As you read the following pieces, notice the historical and cultural baggage that lingers within the young Christians. Notice how their Chinese-ness affects their spiritual development and attitudes towards church and Christianity. Where there is hope, ask yourself what has happened that brought it. Where there is despair, examine the causes.

Allow me to introduce you to the future....

JERRY LIN

Jerry Lin is a twenty-year-old American-born Chinese who grew up in Houston, Texas. His parents are Taiwanese who immigrated to the United States in the 1960s. His father is a non-practicing Buddhist. His mother is a Christian who sent him to Sunday School when he was young in order to teach him good morals. He started growing in the Christian faith in the fourth grade and continued throughout junior high. However, during his high school years, he began to question his faith. This honest doubting process continued into college. Now, he is being discipled by a friend of his brother's who is teaching him from the Bible. He is currently attending an Anglo church because the teaching there is excellent. He feels that the Chinese church he attended before was unsatisfactory in the area of teaching its congregation. They were merely concerned with pragmatic areas, such as, how to behave in church. As a result, the "(church) body suffers."

The following is a piece written by Jerry concerning his identity as a Christian and as a Chinese-American:

I want to start with the question: who are you?

Four years ago, this was a meaningless question for me. See, a friend had asked if I was struggling with that issue and I responded that the question did not lend itself to any extensions... why, I am Jerry Lin. Who is that underneath? That is easy — it is Jerry Lin underneath. And, that was that. Later on, when thinking about it more, thinking about what it meant to be a Chinese-American, I came upon the model that my identity is like a big circle, and within that circle are many sub-circles. For example, most importantly, I am a Christian, so maybe that is the biggest bubble. Then, I suppose I am American, but... I have Chinese roots too, so I guess it would be more precise to say that being Chinese-American is another circle; within that there might be American and Chinese sub-divisions. Then, we might throw in some flavor of my "place" in this world... currently a student, right? I happen to have grown up in Houston, and now I am here at Stanford... That description seemed to make sense to me back then, even up until this summer.

I now believe that I lacked true identity. I am like a shadow ... my contour being formed by the many things in this society, and besides the simple coincidence that society has successfully attached these labels to me, I lacked anything to glue together these random snippets that defined my life. In some sense, I am not an individual, but rather a synthesis, a hodge-podge assemblage of scattered pieces of identity. After all, what happens? Society steps into our lives and says, "You are a student. Of course your primary responsibility in college is to learn and to make good grades." Society might say, "You are an American. Of course you should support democracy, human rights, and capitalism." Or, "You are a Stanford student now. You should make the most of the opportunity and learn as much about computers as you can." Perhaps, though, it is not always this nebulous, ubiquitous societal monster; perhaps a church, or a fellowship, whispers, "You are an AACFer (Asian American Christian Fellowship member) Christian. You should come and do these things." In essence, that our identity is formed by those around us and in the end, we can expect that that drives us crazy with enormous expectations and roles, because, quite frankly, we do not know who we are.

But then, some people do have at least a nominal idea about who they are and what is important to them, but they have not quite taken the time to really find out what that is about, and so sometimes, when someone says something and attaches the right name, they might cling to it ... even if what was promoted is actually against their identity. Some things only seem to promote an idea; it may actually be a hindrance.

It ends up that, without a clear concept of identity or a strong resolution to keep to what is important to us, we very well might try to assimilate another new piece, try to conform to another role, another ideal. And we become increasingly shaped.

I believe society moves to define us in at least two ways:

Although we generally would like to believe that what we believe shapes what we do, that is, we act only in accordance with who we are at heart, sociologists tell us that it is often the opposite. They say that in actuality, although we might first subscribe to a certain system of beliefs, we might do something against our beliefs. Faced with the dilemma of an action inconsistent with who we are, we rationalize, we re-interpret our former value system and adjust our beliefs to eliminate our hypocrisy. For example, years ago, before I started driving, I firmly believed that speeding was downright wrong; it broke the law and therefore was sinning. Soon after I started driving, however, I realized how hard it was to always try and keep the speed limit, and so I became increasingly comfortable about speeding. Realizing this, I began to rationalize and then soon, "Oh, speeding isn't that bad; you need to go with the flow of traffic." The implications of this are enormously scary. It is all too often that we hear the unthoughtful hint that, "Well, everyone else is doing that. Why shouldn't you?" But with the adoption of another habit might come an adoption of another belief.

The other method society uses to mold our identity is through a system of default assumptions. For example, does honoring parents directly map to obedience? Is a forty-hour work week optimal? Does it really leave enough time to care for others? How about the thought that technological progress is always good? How about the assumption that we should be patriotic and always vote? These are just some default assumptions that go widely unchallenged. And as such, they settle in so easily and another part of us becomes defined.

Both of these avenues, as subtle as they might seem, can do a lot in forming who we are.

Before I go on, let us take a look at the concept of identity. What can we reference? Or, perhaps, what is identity and why is it important and what does it communicate?

I think it is helpful to understand "pieces" of identity in terms of labels. For example, I am considered a Chinese-American, so that might be a label that is applied to me. But what about labels? Does it mean that just because someone can apply a label to me that I have to therefore adopt that into my self-perception? The person who does, the person who believes his identity is but a bubble filled with random snippets of what is around, has submitted himself and has allowed himself to be defined by those around him.

Well, what is the nature of a label? Some labels, I believe, are descriptive, or circumstantial. For example, I feel that, in some sense, I happen to have black hair, or that I happen to have spent a lot of time in Houston. These things are not what are important to me; they are just circumstantial. However, some things are much more important to people than, "Oh, I happen to have that." And we see the emergence of a defining label. A defining label provides direction; where there is a relevant issue that we might be confused about, we align ourselves with it. We might take the simple example of the student who feels that his identity is wrapped up in achieving good grades: if he were right about to settle into a nice juicy TV show when he needed time to study for that upcoming midterm, his identity provides guidance for the decision as to whether or not to continue watching. For that student to continue watching TV would be inconsistent with who he is. In that sense, a defining label resolves many decisions because many decisions involve that issue of identity.

Now, some people might take a label to be a defining label while others might take the same label as circumstantial. For example, I feel that, in some sense, I happen to be Chinese-American; someone else might feel that that is what is important to him, that is who he is. So, when he comes upon something that might act against his interest in being Chinese-American, it is a clear choice for him. For me, on the other hand, it is not so clear; I would have to evaluate the decision through other lenses.

Thus, the person who believes his identity is a bubble filled with various labels has taken many things to define him and so has grasped nothing as his identity, of what is important to him — he allows himself to be defined by society. Very quickly, we can predict conflict. For example, what shall the Chinese-American say if China and America were to compete in the Olympics head to head? Or if a man wants to be an industrious worker and loving husband, what shall he do when his supervisors require him to spend more time at work to finish a project, yet his wife is about to deliver a child? See, there is a big problem when we do not know who we fundamentally are. Society, or those around us, steps in and tells us what we should do, or what we should value. "Why, you are a guy, so of course you are supposed to be insensitive" or "You are an American, it is *your* civic responsibility to vote..." "Why, you are my son, you are to become a doctor..." And with each of these that we acquiesce to, we try to assimilate yet another role into our lives, and at least another aspect of our lives is more concretely defined. The problem is, with so many different voices, with so many callings, these different pieces of identity contend for center stage, to be able to overrule any opposing voice. And then, we have the identity crisis ... when we start to realize that we cannot possibly appease all these different voices in our lives and we struggle over which to grant prominence to. My guess is that, ultimately, there can only be one defining label, or else there will probably be strong conflict on some level.

We must choose something to be the defining pillar of our individual identity and let everything else fall into place in relation to it. Then, we can start evaluating decisions without an overwhelming deluge of considerations; our primary considerations will be focused on deciding whether it is consistent with who we are at the core. We might take up the story of a certain someone whom we will call "J", who is Asian-American. "J" grew up and did well in school, pleasing her parents in many ways. Somewhere along the way, she accepted Christ. And on and on she grew. And as she approached the age around which people get married, she too began to notice potential suitors. After some time, she met a wonderful person, and they began dating. Then, her parents found out. The problem was, he did not quite meet the expectations of her parents. His salary was not high enough. His formal education did not match hers. He was of a different Asian descent. He had this "irksome habit" of wanting to help the poor. And we might imagine what she was thinking... where do her primary loyalties lie? What place shall she grant the expectations and wishes of her parents and those of her boyfriend? And what about her cultural ties? It is expected that she end the relationship with him because, after all, he is of *that* descent. And so it is not that hard to imagine all these different voices contending for center stage, leading us back to the questions of who really are we. See, if "J" did not have a clear idea of who she fundamentally was, she might have suffered the prolonged agony posed by the questions of an identity crisis. Listening to only one, deciding what is ultimately important to us, and who we are can make things so much easier; then we can rest, knowing that it is not necessary to please so many people at the same time.

What then shall we choose to answer the question of who are we?

As much as we might like to reference ourselves as the basis for our identity, like I tried to do four years ago, I feel that that is invalid. For one thing, we continue to grow and develop. So, it communicates nothing to my audience when I say that, at heart, I am Jerry Lin because I can be Jerry Lin today and will still be Jerry Lin tomorrow, but I might have changed according to some standard in the meantime. To say that I am Jerry Lin at the core communicates nothing of that change. Since I am a Computer Science major, I am told, it is bad form to recursively define something without a base case to terminate the sequence; that is like trying to explain that an allegory is an ... allegory. That simply does not help my audience understand me any better. That is to say, for me to say that I am Jerry Lin really communicates nothing, not only because I might have changed, but also because it tells nothing of what I am like. Unless, of course, I claim myself to be the ultimate standard and other standards change in reference to me. As much as I might like to think that, that is just not true; I do not define the universe. But, if I were to say at least that, at core, I live solely for my own pleasure, that is something that is already understood between my audience and me, and therefore communicates something. So, in essence, we must reference something beyond ourselves, some idea or some person.

Okay, so what can people identify themselves as?

Some people try to reference ethnic identity. But in this

increasingly multi-cultural society, ethnic identity changes, and the changing ideal poses difficult problems. Those who base their identity on something that changes may often find themselves feeling the tension of leaving what is behind to take hold of what is ahead. Furthermore, that person who clings to his or her ethnic identity is subject to the other person who is able to redefine what ethnic identity means.

Perhaps some live for family. Perhaps there exists children who live to meet their parents' expectations, yet they are unaware of it. Or, don't the lives of some parents revolve around those of their children?

Perhaps some live for a significant other. Does Jane exist in our minds only as John's girlfriend — does she find her identity and fulfillment in that relationship?

There are also those who live for the praise of people. We note that some strive and strive, hoping to achieve that promotion, to climb the corporate ladder, playing games to curry the favor of their supervisors.

Some people find their identity in Christian-y things. James Thomas, paraphrasing John Bunyan, wrote, "With too many, Christianity is but little more than a custom, or a name." I think there can be a large difference between the man who firmly believes and finds it important that, "I am a Protestant" versus the person who insists that he is Christian, and oh, his views happen to coincide with a package that others call Protestant. Fellowship. I sometimes get the feeling that if some people were to discover a Christian did not regularly attend a Christian fellowship, they might gasp in exaggerated appall, "What?!? He is not attending a fellowship? Is he okay? Is his spiritual life suffering?" As if attendance at, and association with a formal fellowship is crucial to our spiritual growth. In reality, I believe the fellowship we attend is just a footnote in relation to our identity in Christ. I am a Christian, and oh, I happen also to be an AACFer. Just like, I happen to be a student now, I happen to be from Houston, I happen to be considered Chinese. At core, though, and what really matters, is that I am a Christian.

It is interesting to note how the Old Testament identifies people. First, we can try to understand how important a name was back then... the name was taken to be an accurate description of the person. For example, Jacob means "he deceives," Joshua means "the Lord saves," and Abraham means "father of many" or "exalted father." So, the Old Testament uses the name to identify someone, and the name itself means something and was supposed to be an accurate encapsulation of identity. But, interestingly, the Old Testament attaches epithets such as, "Joshua son of Nun" or "David son of Jesse" or "Saul son of Kish." Here we see that the Old Testament, in addition to providing the name, references someone who already existed, someone from whom the person is to have derived his nature. So, I believe that when Moses asked God who he was and God responded "I am who I am" (Exodus 3:14), I believe that God was making a claim about himself. First, that he is constant and does not change. We see this in James 1:17. Next, I believe he is also claiming that he is the first, that there is no one and nothing before him that he could reference, even if he wanted to; that is, he is the center of the universe, from which all others derive their standing. Paul makes this point in Ephesians 3:14-15. Third, because he exists, because he has preceded us, because his existence is meaningful and is known by others, I believe others can reference him.

And, Christians do. God is the Christian's defining pillar of identity.

But so often, it seems like people, including Christians, mistake what being a Christian involves; people sometimes seem

24

to think that when a person becomes a Christian, God becomes a helper to help them excel in certain areas of life. Or, don't some people buy into the statement that Christians must perform, not for God, but for others that they might be a powerful witness, not through who they are, but rather, what they do ... like the assumption that the Christian student is called to work hard to achieve high grades? People might think that being a Christian makes them more moral, more responsible, better students, more active citizens... It is as if some people believe that Christians must beat the world in its own game to be an effective testimony of God's abundant riches. But, in reality, when they accept Christ, God is not their helper to excel in the world's eyes, in what the world values; when they accept Christ, God redefines their core by coming to dwell inside them by his Spirit. Paul writes, "I pray that out of his glorious riches he may strengthen you with power through his Spirit in your inner being, so that Christ may dwell in your hearts through faith" (Ephesians 3:16). Ezekiel prophesied about this with the Lord saying, "I will sprinkle clean water on you, and you will be clean; I will cleanse you from all your impurities and from all your idols. I will give you a new heart and put a new spirit in you; I will remove from you your heart of flesh. And I will put my Spirit in you and move you to follow my decrees and be careful to keep my laws" (Ezekiel 36:25-27). Paul, drawing on what it meant to have Christ incarnated in us writes, "Or do you not know that your body is a temple of the Holy Spirit who is in you?" (1 Corinthians 6:19). Paul says, "I have been crucified with Christ; and it is no longer I who live, but Christ lives in me" (Galatians 2:20). Notice the contrast: the others that want to define us just stand outside of us and issue demands and expectations to be met; Christ is the only one that meets us where we are and works in us to transform us. Jesus himself said that when Christians partake in him, he comes and dwells in them: "Whoever

25

eats my flesh and drinks my blood remains in me, and I in him" (John 6:56). It is clear that Christ lives in Christians through the Holy Spirit, and that is who a Christian is.

So, what does this mean for us? God lives in us, individually and specifically. No longer do we need to distance ourselves from our beliefs by timidly prefacing our strong statements with, "Well, as a Christian, I believe..." this or that. No, we are Christians — that is who we are, that is what we believe; we can assert with great confidence that what God has told us is the truth. When Christians read the Bible, no longer do they need to say, "Aha! Look at this good man. I desire to be like him." We were not just given an awesome model of love and ethics to struggle to imitate. No, Christ is in all Christians. When we read of Jesus' boldness before all people, when we read how Jesus had compassion, when we read of his amazing love, we can say, "That is who I am." To muddle our identity with anything of this world, to try and achieve a "balanced" life of this world would be a compromise that would lead to disastrous results. As Dormon Followwill used to so powerfully assert, "Christianity is an all-or-nothing proposition."

Our acceptance of Christ is an enormous transformation redefining us from our center... This has multiple implications:

Knowing who we are can prevent us from finding our identity in the wrong places. When I was young, I was told to be proud of my Chinese heritage because I was Chinese. For a period of time, I did grow up to be proud of being Chinese. Now, however, being a bit more mature, I can see that as a framework for supporting racism. I need not find my identity in that any longer... there are more important things.

When confronted with an issue of sin, we can squarely face the question, and firmly respond, "That is not who I am." That is a powerful measure of resisting sin.

Furthermore, understanding this is freedom. No longer do we need to be bound to serving the world or the world's values. Knowing who we are can prevent the trap of the Pharisees from coming upon us: John commented that they "loved praise from men more than praise from God" (John 12:43). There is only one voice to listen to; we no longer need to be shackled by the constant oppression of fulfilling the expectations and obeying the cries of those around us. Jesus said, "You will know *the truth*, and the truth shall set you *free*" (John 8:32). We simply do not need to fill the world's mold.

With all of that in mind, we are prepared to answer that crucial question: Who are we? Each of us who is a Christian has been given a new identity, an identity far more exciting than anything anyone here could possibly come up with: God is in us and we are the salt and the light of the world (Matthew 5).

KEITH CHAU

Keith is a nineteen-year-old second generation ABC college student. His mother is from Guangdong, and his father is from Hong Kong. His mother is a Christian, and she brought Keith to church (his current church) at a very young age. He developed a faith in Jesus Christ during the end of his junior high years and into the beginning of his high school years. However, he never became very involved with the church. The only reason he stayed at church is for his family's sake and for social purposes. If not for these two reasons, Keith would not have had anything to do with the church.

Throughout his church life, Keith experienced much that has turned him off. Policies established by the leaders at church, the hypocrisy of the "respected" members of the congregation, political games, and power-

tripping authorities, had left him cynical and rather jaded by the church culture.

The following is a conversation I had with him regarding his attitude towards his church:

Why do you go (to church)?

Primarily for social reasons, secondarily for family obligations. I do not go to service ... If you come at me twice with church stuff, it gets kinda out of focus, I do not think I can hack it with both church and Sunday school. It is good for people who are really into it, but for me I do not think ... I do not really like going to worship.

When was the last time you went to worship?

Last week, but that was the first time in about three months.

What did you think of it?

It's cool, but sometimes it gets out of hand with all the stories, but if that is the way the pastor preaches then that is the way he should preach it ... sometimes it is gonna be an attention grabber, sometimes not.

Does it grab your attention?

Only when it is stories I have not heard.

Have you heard most of the stories?

Oh yeah! Been there that long, probably have heard most of the stories.

Speaking of stories, tell me a story of a time you have been frustrated.

Lot of times I've been frustrated...A lot of times it is like...why would they want to do a stupid thing like that?

Like what?

You know how they are re-doing the church building. I do not see why they have to. A reason why is for looks. It is all based on what you have, what you own, how big it is... that is the way I see it.

It just kind of gets to me...how a church can spend so much. And you know...how you figure a church can make so much? Look at the pastors, they look pretty well-off. I am not saying that pastors should not be getting paid, I am just saying that it is weird to see them having all this stuff. For example, Rev. _____ he's got all the new Nikes, all the new toys...always got something new.

What about the Steve incident? You told me earlier of an incident during high school in which a pastor specifically told you and a group of your friends not to hang out with a guy named Steve because he was a "bad influence" since he left the church. Talk about that...

What the (expletive) was going on?!?!? The Steve incident was frustrating. Blown way out of proportion.

And then another thing is about partying and dancing...That was such a trip...that was way out of hand. Right when they started about that...

You lost interest?

Yeah. And another thing, I know that Rev. _____ favors a certain group of people.

Why them?

They are a bunch of dorks and they are clique-ish...But Rev. _____ really favors them because they are into certain stuff and he likes that...

Tell me more about the favoritism...

Well, it is just like what I said, I mean, like the class above me, they are into basketball, so Rev. _____ favors them. They are on the basketball team. They got the talent. When other people come in, they do not get the playing time (on the church basketball team). It is just that one class. The whole class. How ya gonna tell me that there is no one else that is just as good?

Has anyone ever complained about this?

(Expletive) yeah!

Oh really...

People quit because of that, man! People quit because of that. I mean, they will play for the love of the sport, but they will fool around to show rebellion, to rebel against them, y'know. That is what I did. A lot of people realize it now; a lot of people opened their eyes to it. Like, I was talking to this guy the other day, and he was like, "Yeah, I see it too." I said, "Man, you need to open your eyes, and see what type of church you are going to." We were just talking, and I just said, "A lot of times you see this (favoritism) and you just have to open your eyes." And it finally hit him and he said, "Oh yeah, that is right, it is true." Everything that I said, he saw. And I told him, "But do not let me persuade you about how you feel about church, or else they are gonna blame me for turning you away." You really need to open your eyes...

I felt this way for a long time, but I did not want to say nothing because I did not want to off-track people. I did not want to take them away because I thought that everyone else was happy.

When did you first realize this?

When my friend Sam left. His point of view is that he believes in God. But a person should not have to do all these things just to get along with everybody else. When he started to realize it, I began to look at the overall picture. I was not agreeing with a lot of things that were happening at church. First of all, the Steve incident, the (no)-dancing policy, and a lot of other stuff. Why? What is the problem (with hanging out with Steve)? We chose to do our own thing, and they are just trying to look for someone to blame. They did not want to go off right away and say, "O.K. you guys are a bad class." I thought they were just looking for someone to blame it on, and that is the way it seemed. They partially blamed dancing and partying on Steve because he was there. They are using him as a scapegoat just to talk away all the things that were said about us, or thought about us.

Any more stories?

Yeah, this one time at volleyball. Gordon (a church leader), man, I was about to hit him. He told me, "Hey, spit out your gum!" Everybody chews gum in the gym, but he specifically targeted me. Everybody else was chewing gum. That is favoritism right there. What was the point of that? Was it just to bust me out in front of everybody? Out of 30-something people that were there? What was the point of that?

Are you still talking to him?

NO! Why would I talk to that (expletive) for?!?

Just asking...

He is a (expletive) at the store (where I work with him) too. He bought me lunch, right? Afterwards, he said he had to let me go. I was fired and he turns around and hires Hank's girlfriend.

Are you kidding?!?

What kind of (expletive) is that? I worked there the whole summer and then he says, "I'm gonna have to let you go." I said, "Fine, just give me my money and I'm out." Then a few weeks later, Hank's girlfriend started working there. How the (expletive) ya gonna tell me that I did not do a good job? I did all the hard labor. All them (expletive) boxes and (expletive) like that! How ya gonna tell me I did not do a good job? I was the one sweating in the back room while they were fooling around. I was getting six dollars an hour. How ya gonna tell me I did not do a (expletive) good job? I was the one who reorganized the (expletive) boxes. They are heavy, man!

Did you go back and say anything to him?

No, I would just take discounts and take things from them... to compensate for all my hard work. All the Pringles. Pringles and Chapstick, y'know what I'm saying?

Back to the subject of your church experience...

I got the black file.

Come again???

I am black-listed there. Laurence, my college sponsor, even knew I smoked and did all these things.

How did he know?

No idea. I said to him, "What do you know about me? What do they say about me?" He said, "What I know is that you smoke, that you go to parties." I was like, where do you get this stuff? It is like a Watergate up there.

Matt, my other sponsor, took me out to dinner one day, and I just told him how I felt. I did not give a (expletive) anymore. I was not gonna play along and say, "Cool, my life is great. I am doing devotions. I am doing everything." I said, "I did not give a (expletive) about church no more. A lot of things I do not agree with. This is my opinion, so do not knock me for it." He was...he actually understood what I was saying.

Church is a very governmental society. It is all about who has the power and who has the authority. If you want to hear the truth, I will tell you the truth. It is all about authority and power. That is basically the truth. It is all about power; that is how it is at church — power and politics. That is the way church is. Can't do nothing about it.

If you got money, that equals power. They automatically give it to you.

Have you seen it around your church?

You can tell. Look at all these people driving high-priced Volvo's, BMW's, and Benz's. Money buys it. It is guaranteed. If you tithe well, they treat you with respect. Mr. _____, that's money right there. That's bank. And look how powerful he is around church.

And Mr. _____, look how he is balling at church. Money gets you up there. Authority, power, and now money.

So power, authority, and money, huh?

The three things that get you power in the Chinese community, gets you power in the Chinese church. You know why? Because money is such an important thing to Chinese people. I mean, that is like the main thing. Look how they want you to succeed. To succeed is to have lots of money. Succeeding nowadays to us is having a good job and making it, not just necessarily making ends meet, being well-off enough so that you have your own house or apartment, or whatever. You are not living off the welfare of your parents. Succeeding for Chinese is like ... money. It is all about money ...

And a German car?

A Rolex watch. All the fantasies the Chinese people have. When you see that at church... Name a person at your church who does not drive a nice car.

Hmmm...

Mmm Hmm...

NATALIE LEONG

Natalie Leong is a twenty-four-year-old second generation Chinese-American, and a third generation Christian. Both her parents were born in China and immigrated to the United States during the 1960s wave of immigration after the Exclusionary Act was repealed. They met at the University of California at Berkeley at a dance and were eventually married. Natalie was born in 1973 in San Francisco where she now lives. Her paternal grandfather became a Christian as a teenager through the work of American missionaries who taught him English in the 1930s. However, her father, for some reason, became anti-Christian and anti-organized religion. Her maternal grandmother was a Christian who raised her daughter (Natalie's mother) as a Methodist. Natalie's mother eventually became a devoted member of a Chinese church in San Francisco.

This is the church where Natalie was raised in since age seven. She remembers having a bad attitude ("B.A.") when she was in junior high, at school, and at church. She acted like a "rebel" in order to compensate for feelings of inferiority and a low self-esteem. However, during her eighth grade year, she gradually developed a relationship with Christ and her bad attitude went away. She learned to like herself for who she was. She realized that God loves her and that he can change people.

As a result, she began to get more involved in her church as she entered high school. She loved her church and saw it as "utopia" during her freshman year. But that feeling of euphoria regarding her church went away as quickly as it came. She did not fit in with the other high school kids at the church. She felt that she was different. Her rebellious side re-emerged. Influenced by movies such as The Breakfast Club and Fast Times at Ridgemont High, she wanted more excitement than she thought that her church could provide, especially since she did not get along with her fellowship group. When she was sixteen years old, she got a weekend job at the zoo just so that she would have an excuse not to go to fellowship meetings and worship services. The only reason she even

35

kept any ties to the church was because of her mother ("My mother, and the guilt that she put on me, kept me there!"). Her familial obligation to please her mother was the only thing that held the obligations of her church over her head.

She "endured" and "suffered through" her church life for the next few years. Finally, upon graduating from college, she made a decision to leave the church she had grown up in. It was a difficult period in her spiritual journey. There was a need for healing, for personal revival, for a new church, and for her to let go of a great deal of bitterness. She found all of this while on an InterVarsity-run retreat on Catalina Island. Here is the letter she wrote to the InterVarsity group after the retreat:

November 7, 1996

Dear I.V.,

I have been composing this letter in my head for some time. (How flattered you must be to know that I'm still thinking about the retreat.) Now I am more than compelled to write, since I just got off the phone with my old High School Fellowship leader, Vivian. Viv was very active in I.V. back in college, and knew "that joy" that comes with reading the Bible, digging deeper into his Word, and praying earnestly and intensely.

As far as my spiritual growth, by the end of summer, I had left my old church of fifteen years because of continuous disappointment and dissatisfaction; happily found a new one, thanks to my cousin (been there for two months now), and gone to an AACF (Asian American Christian Fellowship) meeting at UCLA, one week prior to the retreat. I went to the retreat without any expectations ... well, except that I wanted to see how other Christians worshipped, especially college students.

Since junior year, I had hardened my heart to anything religiously oriented. After all, being in news (as a journalism student), I'm very aware of what the social issues, current events and moods are. I grew cynical of organized religion. How could I not? Operation Rescue claimed it was a sin to kill babies, yet they killed the doctors who performed abortions?! The Branch Davidians claimed David Koresh of Waco, Texas was their Messiah? The Christian Coalition went on a witch hunt against books written by people of color?! Or the KKK, who claimed they were doing God's work by ridding the nation of blacks, Hispanics, and Jews. The Religious Right donated thousands of dollars into Pat Buchanan or Phil Gramm's presidential campaign — when there is a Federal law that prohibits churches from doing just that! Not to mention, those weirdo Church of Christ cultists and Moonies that always seemed to approach me whenever I was by myself on campus. The sandwich-board preacher that came to campus to condemn us for being heathens. He drew an angry mass crowd, that yelled back in scorn and chanted "Racist, Sexist, Anti-gay, Christian Bigot, Go Away!" Such embarrassing actions ... I was so ashamed to let people know I shared their values and beliefs. In the past few years, I didn't tell people I was a Christian. And I wondered...was God a loving, but just God? Or had people gone overboard by interpreting God's law as they saw fit to their own agenda?

I had trouble fitting in with my old church. The college department is very conservative. And uniform, too. There's a certain image you've just got to have in order to blend in. And because I believed that what's inside is more important than your physical appearance, I never conformed to their plain-jane "dress code." So being eccentric, I had a hard time accepting that you could still be cool like your friends at school, and still be an active believer.

Those three days on Catalina Island have made a big difference in my life. Those three days restored my faith in Christianity, in God's heart, in God's people, and that not all organized religion is quirky. Everyone was so unique, from all walks of life, and yet shared a common bond — the bond of love.

37

I had never been so spiritually enthralled before. You are an amazing testimony to God ... the people involved with I.V. are growing, are on fire for the Lord, and accept others just as they are. And like a non-Christian searching for purpose in life, I wanted that special joy. I wanted to be part of "this thing" that made everyone glow from within ...

Singing praises with a room full of people who actually love to sing praises was so uplifting ... in songs like *We Exalt Thee, Jesus Is Lord*, and *Father of Lights*. People didn't clap to keep rhythm — they clapped for joy. Watching people raise their arms in sweet surrender was inspiring. The room rocked, and I undoubtedly felt the Spirit amongst us. And the voices ... singing with such passion and soul! For the first time ever, I closed my eyes and lifted my hands to the Lord while singing praises. What an awesome feeling it was — to really feel the Spirit moving within me ... And although I didn't know half the songs, just watching the motivated worship team was enough to prove to any non-believer that the mighty presence of God was indeed there.

And small group Bible study ... you'll get that warm and fuzzy feeling when I tell you how incredible it was to dig so deeply into both The Prodigal Son and the Good Samaritan. Initially I thought, how elementary ... I've known these stories since I was in fourth grade. But I never picked at them or questioned what actually was going on, the way English literature classes dissect stories and poetry... character study, attitudes, historical context, the culture, and identity are all pertinent to understanding the essence of what is really being taught. I've never been asked who I'm more like — the older brother or the prodigal son ... after I shared, I realized I was venting out my frustrations of being the "cream of the Oreo cookie."

The sermons of love, particularly unconditional love ... Had I received it? Had I even practiced that? I've tried ... but you can only be a martyr for so long. I wondered ... in 23 years of living, had I ever experienced unconditional love? I can answer, quite affirmatively, Yes. The times I slandered the Christian faith, when I badmouthed my former church, when I pretended to like the people in my fellowship, yet gossiped behind their backs, whenever I spoke and behaved hedonistically, and wanted to have nothing to do with church. Sometimes I wondered when God would strike me down for being so bold and callused. Instead of punishing me, God provided a new church, suited to my ideal, took me to an AACF meeting, and blessed me at the retreat. God has been so good to me ...

JACOB LAU

Jacob Lau is a second generation ABC. His parents are immigrants from Taiwan who raised Jacob and his sister in a strict but loving Christian home. He was forced to play the violin at a very early age (and play it well), was forbidden to watch television, and could only play Nintendo on "special occasions." He recalled instances of secretly watching television while his parents were out; he had to place cold ketchup bottles from the refrigerator on top of the television to cool it down so that his mother would not detect that the television had been used.

His parents brought him to church ever since he was born. Jacob was raised a Christian. He was obligated to show up at all the church functions as a familial duty. He was expected to "perform" as a good Chinese Christian boy during all the church meetings that his parents attended. He vividly remembered having to pray in front of everyone in Taiwanese. Even more vividly, Jacob remembered dreading those moments. He learned to constantly be at his best while at church. He never questioned anything during his youth.

However, as he entered high school and college, he began to question his faith in God, in Christ, and in the church. He started to wonder if he had just put on a show his whole life in order to retain social harmony with his family and the other people at his church. Having gone off to college, he is now on his own. Jacob now has the independence to make choices concerning his future and his faith. This uncertainty is both refreshing and frightening. Wonderfully bizarre, yet despairingly complex. He now watches as much TV as he wants to.

The following is a conversation I had with Jacob Lau concerning his Christian development:

Your family background...

My parents are pretty much classic Taiwanese parents.

What are "classic Taiwanese parents?" What do you mean by that?

They are ... they strive to be insensitive, I think.

Strive to be insensitive?!?

Because the more insensitive the parents are, as viewed by other parents, the more successful you are. Insensitive in the sense that they do not care for their kid's feelings; they have total control over them. They do not give their kids leeway. Obedience from the kids is highly regarded.

So obedience and insensitivity are inter-related?

I guess I should change the word "insensitivity" to "control."

Control, ahhh...

Right, domineering, which can be played off as insensitive, I think so.

Back to your family...

My dad is pure Taiwanese. There is a lot of controversy about being 100% Taiwanese. From Taiwan, a farmer boy. Fabulously Formosan ... alliteration. He grew up on a farm, and he was the only one in his family to make any kind of success, to make it to the United States. His dad died early and his mom sat at home and did nothing. Actually, my father told me that his father barely knew him; he just worked most of the day. Very utilitarian relationship. It was like ... I feed you, therefore I am a good father. He (my father) was very successful at school. He had an inner passion to get away from the farm. He hated the farming life; he wanted to get out.

My mom was born in Taiwan, too. She was really well-off, from the upper crust. Her dad was in the import/export business. Her mother became a Christian. They were a tight family, so my mom became a Christian, too.

My dad was not a Christian, but my mom was. There was a lot of controversy. Everyone in my mom's church was like, "What are you doing with him? You can't do that!" So they got married against the will of a lot of people. Eventually he came around and became a Christian after five to ten years. My dad used to smoke and drink and do a lot of bad stuff. But things changed.

So what kind of environment did you grow up in? What was family life like?

Family life was very Christian ... very Christian. Very stereotypical Asian Christian family. There are those. I went to a Taiwanese church. Everyone was very close. Everyone knew everyone else. They have family get-togethers. Very tight, and non-evangelistic. My parents brought me to church every Sunday. They even took me to their family Bible meetings where I was the only kid. They made me pray in front of everybody ... in Taiwanese, of course. Very traumatic.

41

Looking back, do you think you benefited from this, or is it just a traumatic childhood experience that you would rather throw away?

Overall, I think my parents did a good thing. Oh, and my parents sent me to a Christian school. They really stressed the importance of learning at a Christian school. My mom was a Sunday School teacher; she was very strict. At my church, she was scary. Everyone was scared of her. So everyone respects me for living with her. But she was not as bad at home though. She was just "mommy" at home.

So you grew up in a very authoritarian household. Tight ship. What about your own spiritual development? Your Christian awareness?

I grew up in the church. Every church has one of those kids who knew all the Bible stories, knows all the books of the Bible, the star of the Sunday School.

That was you?

Yeah...

Hey, you even prayed in Taiwanese...

You know it! Yep, prayed in Taiwanese. I had "all the right answers." And even when I did not answer right, the teacher would go, "OK, yeah, sure..." He probably did not know the answer either.

OK, so you were being forced to go to church on Sundays, but when was the first time you asked yourself, "What is this all about?"

I think I was a late one. It probably happened to me freshman year.

Of high school?

Mmm hmm...

So in eighth grade, you were going because it was a family thing, and then what happened after that?

Well, I went to a Taiwanese church. The pressure, every Sunday. A lot of social pressure. I felt obligated to go to everything and put on a show. Remember, I was Mr. Sunday School. It was not easy. Then, we switched churches. My parents feared that ... well, the high school fellowship was pretty weak at my old church.

So they switched churches because of you?

Yeah, mostly me. Then, I had an epiphany sophomore year.

What happened?

I got baptized sophomore year. But I did not know what the (expletive) I was doing. I had a hard time just believing.

What was going on inside your head? You just switched churches and you just got baptized. But...

Because ... I felt like I had been brainwashed. All my life, it was church church church. I always hung out at church. Now I am in high school, surrounded by non-Christian people ... everywhere. A variety of people. Christianity was given to me kind of as a paradigm for operating in my family life and social life.

Hmm...

So during my baptism, I gave my testimony to the church. I felt so fake...

You felt fake at the time, or in retrospect, you know you were fake?

I think in retrospect, but at the time I thought I was a good Christian boy, who was doing the right thing.

So what was your testimony? Can you give a synopsis?

Contrary to the fascinating testimonies of non-Christians who convert, mine was rather dry, you know. I just said, you know, everything I already told about my family and growing up in the chruch. My parents ... taught me well.

And finally, during my freshman/sophmore years, I guess that was when my brain started working. I began to question all these "facts." Why did I know them? Does it really matter? I just believed them because I am who I am.

Then, I saw *A Thief in the Night* and I had nightmares.

A Thief in the Night... that Christian movie about the end times and the rapture and all that?

Yeah that one. I remained in the faith because of fear. That is why my faith is really weak right now.

Wow ... that is very honest of you. I appreciate that. It is rather refreshing.

I do think God is real. Me reading the Bible at night, doing personal devotions. I think there is something there. Something hits me. After sophmore year, I grew quite a bit. But senior year was the big fallout.

What's the deal with senior year?

I sat in Sunday School, I sat in service, and I sat in choir. Choir was just a disaster. They cannot sing so they try to find other things to do, like argue. They would cause a lot of trouble, and then be all nice and stuff and say, "Hi-yee, glad you could make it to choir!!!" (laughs)

Hmm...

After a while, I am like "Been there, done that, seen that, heard that, thank you very much, goodbye." Oh, yeah. I didn't even know why I was there. Hated it...

So what happened in your senior year that disappointed you? Was it a specific event, or was it a gradual process?

Well, it was a process. But I remember this one time at fellowship, the guy, the leader, he did not have a Bible lesson planned, so he just asked us to pick a book from the Bible, like a letter from Paul or something. He was like, "Alright, let's just pick a book, people." Ho-hum... Geez.... That's how ho-hum it got.

Ho-hum, hmm?

So I stopped going.

You stopped going?

Well, on and off.

OK now you're in college, how are you doing now?

I am going to a Taiwanese church right now. I have no problem saying "hi" to people there. But the thing that bothers me about this church is that you have to be this type of person, do certain things, use certain catch phrases in order to belong in that church. This church that I am going to now ... it is all about assimilation. The way they dress, the way they act, the way they talk. So I don't belong. I can't belong. If you do not conform, they will frown upon you. That is saying to me that in order to be a Christian, you have to act a certain way, you have to ... if you do not go to church one Sunday, they are like, "What is wrong? Don't you like our church?"

How does this affect you personally?

I feel I have to assimilate. I feel like a Black Panther.

You feel like a Black Panther?!?

(laughs violently) I feel like I have to assimilate or die.

What do you think will happen if you are determined to go to church and not conform?

They would just view me totally different. I do not think I can grow at that church.

You would not be able to grow?

No!!!

So it is either conform or leave?

It is either conform or, I hate to say it, be brainwashed and grow, in that sense. But I do not think that is Christian growth; that is just socialization. A lot of things are good; I like what some of the people have to offer. I have high respect for them.

Well, that's good...

But there is a lot of hypocrisy going on in the church. They like to point out the wrongs. The whole point of evangelism ... what is it?

Outreach, right?

Right, but how do they plan to do that if ... it is so hard to break into the inner circle at the church. It gets really frustrating. To get into that inner circle is impossible.

What do you think that they think about you?

I do not think people there are too impressed with me, especially since I do not come to church that often. They do not have the impression of me as a strong Christian. But then again, I would not give myself that credential either. But, I do think that that church is a good church; it is one of the better churches around. I mean, I do not want to be a church basher or anything. I am just being honest.

Yes, you are just being honest.

I am sure every church has its problems. But honestly, I do not get anything out of church. I come out of service and I am like, "What was he (the pastor) talking about?!?" Then, I am like, "Where are we going for lunch?"

You are not content, I imagine...

It would be hard for me to be content.

Do you think you would want to continue going to Chinese churches or are you through with them?

Well, I have considered the alternatives, and I do not like them. I could never see myself at an American church ... and I could never see myself at a purely Chinese church.

Commentary on the Four Interviews

Reverend Sam Chan
Senior Pastor, Richmond Hill Chinese Community Church,
Richmond Hill, Ontario, Canada

Four interviews were presented in this chapter, giving a brief history and the struggle of these young Chinese-Americans. Their struggles included a search for identity, their understanding of the purpose of the church, internalizing their faith, and assimilating into and enjoying the church. We are encouraged by the candid sharing of their intense feelings about their situation, and their courage to try to cope and to arrive at some conclusions.

To understand ourselves, our faith, and the church, we need to know what a true, biblical, functioning community (the church), as designed by God, should be like. We also need to know the differences between God himself, who is the object of our faith, and the things of God, which may be the offspring of our faith. There are vast differences between God and the church, Christ and Christianity, God and theology, and God's ownership and our identity. Many times the latter only bears the name of the former, and at times the latter uses the name of the former in vain.

We are indeed given a new identity in Christ after we are saved. We know who we are because we have come to know whom we belong to. However, let us not become too quick to assume that culture, nationality, ethnic traditions, and so forth, are all products of sin and worldliness. Let us learn some lessons from

Joseph, David, Paul, and Jesus Christ. They were clear about their roles, and their cultural and ethnic background. They realized that all of these had shaped them to know who they are; they sought to live up to their calling and mission because of who they are.

If the church cannot manifest Christ, Christianity is a misrepresentation of Christ. Even theologians have announced the death of God. This, however, does not mean that God does not exist. God exists and lives powerfully in our hearts. If we focus on the behavior of a particular church and certain immature believers, we are bound to be disappointed. We will not believe, nor see God, because our trust and faith is in humankind. We are asking humankind to give us answers about God. When we are discouraged by people, our desperation will drive us to seek God, to ask God, and eventually to know and trust him.

It is time for all the church leaders and theologians to re-think the purpose of the church as defined by the Bible. There are needs and demands from the world to put the church in a certain mold. Yet we must "let the church be the church," to be and to do what God intends her to be. The church exists to consecrate our lives to God; to celebrate the life of God; to cultivate our growth in Christ; to care for one another and for our community; and, to communicate Christ to the world. When the church lives according to her biblical purpose, and learns to prioritize her life in descending order of Purpose, People, Program, and Property, a truly biblical, functioning community will emerge. All leaders and God's people must rally together and humbly reconsider the joy of being the church, and to develop the life of the church.

Reverend Alex Yeung, D. Min.

Senior Pastor, Mississauga Chinese Baptist Church, Mississauga,
Ontario, Canada

The stories of the four American-born Chinese young adults touched my heart. I admire their courage to talk about their feelings, their honesty to reveal their inner struggles with the Chinese churches and their families, as well as their sincerity to question their Christian faith. Chinese churches and families need to listen to their cries if we desire to reach out and minister to our American-born Chinese effectively. They struggle constantly with four major life issues as we hear from their stories.

Images of Success

In the minds of many American-born Chinese young adults, Chinese churches view success just as the world does. Successful churches have big congregations, beautiful church buildings, large spending budgets, and parishioners wearing designer clothes and driving luxury cars. They have professional Sunday worship teams, after-school basketball teams, and summer baseball teams. American-born Chinese young adults often find it hard for them to fit into these subtle images of success projected by Chinese churches. They feel pressured to conform to the expectations of Chinese churches and families for success. On the contrary, the Bible tells us that God has a different set of values for success. The parables of the Ten Virgins, the Talents, and the Sheep and the Goats, tell us that Jesus measures success by *our watchfulness, faithfulness, and charity to the poor and the rejected.*

Authenticity of Spirituality

It is good for Chinese churches and families to promote obedience and filial piety, since the Scriptures teach obedience and

51

respect for our parents. Misunderstanding from the American-born Chinese develops, however, when Chinese church leaders and religious parents emphasize only the institutionally authorized and culturally acceptable behaviors, or the "doing." The Scriptures demand, rather, personal transformation of the attitude, or the "being" of an individual. Authentic spirituality is evangelistic by nature. It is a conversion of one's life instead of an acculturation of one's behavior. It operates on life-transformation more than just behavior-conformation. Jerry raises a controversial yet accurate question when he asks, *"Does honoring parents directly map to obedience?"* Natalie could tell when people perform in worship when they clap their hands just to keep the rhythm. She experiences an authentic worship when people clap for joy and raise their hands to surrender their lives to Jesus as their Lord. *Spiritual doing comes only from Spiritual being.*

Consistency of Christian Lifestyle

We may not like to hear the bad experiences of Jacob and Keith with their church leaders. We may even dismiss them as isolated cases. Their stories, however, are wake-up calls to all of us pastors and leaders of the church. How easy it is for us to offer rhetoric sermons and Sunday School lessons. It is natural for us to shout "pro-life" in front of an abortion clinic. But, it is hard for us to tell the doctor who performs an abortion, "God loves you." The litmus test of our teachings on unconditional love, forgiveness, humility, and commitment, comes in our lifestyle. The ways we relate to the people at work, the underachievers around us, the people on the streets, and our family members, speak volumes to people. Are there cliques in the churches and rebellious youth at home? Perhaps it is time for us pastors, leaders, parents, counselors, and Sunday School teachers to take stock of the consistency in our Christian lifestyle. More humble services and less rhetoric speech are the hardest lifestyle for us leaders and parents to keep up with as role models for the next generation. We need to ask our Lord, the humble servant *par excellence* to grant us grace and wisdom to live a balanced and consistent Christian life.

Reality of Identity

Jerry touches on the fundamental struggle of the American-born Chinese: "Who am I?" He gave a good analysis and clear biblical view on the issue of *identity*. The stories of Natalie, Keith, and Jacob also reflect their inner dilemma of their identity. Are they Chinese, Chinese-American, or Chinese-American Christians? Is there a correct order for these terms? The reality of our identity is always multiple and not single. On the one hand, every human being is a person. On the other hand, a person bears the identity of gender, race, family, ethnicity, nationality, religious faith, and so on. The issue of identity becomes a problem when we place *value* on the identities that one holds. Some identities are better than others. We find it hard to obtain "superior identity" and reject our "inferior identity." We even subconsciously put a person down because of his or her identity. Scripture tells us that God creates all human beings in his own image. Jesus Christ came to redeem human beings from their sins and renew their real BEING, God's image. All men and women, Jews or Gentiles, the free or the slave, are therefore equally invaluable in the eyes of Jesus Christ. For Jesus loves all (see Galatians 3:28). It is mandatory for all Christians holding multiple identities to live out the gospel message of Jesus Christ. Let us learn to reconcile and make peace with one another, disregarding our identities. May we all join our hands and pledge, *"Let there be peace on earth, and let it begin with me."*

Facing the Crises of Our Time

Disappointed, dissatisfied, angry, almost despairing... yet many Chinese-American Christians have a deep respect for God. They are hungry for spiritual things, and for a genuine, loving relationship with God and with God's people.

How did we, the Chinese church in North America, get to this point? And how can we better understand and serve the ABCX generation?

Times of Crises

There are moments in life when a major transition takes place. Such moments may be a move from Asia to North America; marriage; a commitment to Jesus Christ; death of someone we love; a divorce; or, cancer. We know God is changing us in a significant way.

There are moments in the history of a people or nation, which affect millions of lives. Most Chinese Christians were influenced directly or indirectly by the revolution in China in 1949 — it has indirectly caused the emigration of Chinese to Taiwan, Hong Kong, Southeast Asia, and North America. The Cultural Revolution (1966-1976) also permanently changed the psyche of the Chinese people. When a major change occurs, there is no turning back.

There are moments in world history when a major transition takes place, which alters how billions of people think and act. The Renaissance and Reformation in the sixteenth century altered what Europeans (and eventually non-Europeans) thought about God, humanity, and the universe. The Industrial Revolution was another major transition point. World War I was yet another, shattering hopes that technology would bring utopia for humankind.

We are living in one such major transition right now. The sooner we realize the magnitude and profound significance of this global change, the more ready we will be to adjust our thinking, strategy, and relationships, so that we could be effective ambassadors for Jesus Christ in the twenty-first century, reaching out to Generation X, and subsequent generations.

A five hundred-year period, called "the Modern Age," is coming to an end. A two hundred-year period, during which England and the United States dominated the globe with their empire-building, space race, and world impact, is coming to an end. A major intellectual movement, which dominated the world for two hundred fifty years, the "Enlightenment project," is coming to an end. In their place, a vague, formless civilization called "postmodernity" is emerging. "Generation X" is the name we gave to the postmodern young people in our universities and young adulthood today. And in the twenty-first century, China and Asia will play a major global role, economically, politically, and we trust, spiritually. Given Generation X's honesty and hunger for relationships, we have grounds to be optimistic about the future. Yet from another perspective, the very foundations of human civilization are crumbling.

The Crises in Our Time

What are some of the characteristics of this "postmodern age" which is dawning?

Crisis of the Mind. The prophets of postmodernism are teaching our university students about "deconstructionism." This philosophy is taught mostly through literature, art, music, and the media. Put simply, deconstructionism teaches that there is no relationship between a sign (for example, grape juice) and the thing which it signifies (for example, the blood of Jesus Christ). This is true for all things. Words are merely words; they may not point to true facts and objects.

In history and in the real world, facts really do not exist. It is obvious that, based on this kind of irrational view of knowledge, truth does not and cannot exist in the world. It is not possible to have absolute truth. As a matter of fact, the word "truth" is replaced by another word: "narratives." There are different stories, but there is not one eternally true story.

Add to this intellectual confusion (or suicide!) is the fact that American education is failing to produce students who can compete in the world market in mathematics and verbal skills. This has been happening since the early 1980s. In fact, college admission tests such as the Scholastic Aptitude Test (SAT), have been "dumbed down" in order to keep the scores up.

Crisis of the Soul. Postmodern people are often very religious. Postmodernity has its own religions, loosely grouped under the heading of "New Age Spirituality."

The word "God" is used in New Age Spirituality in a way radically different from the way the Bible uses it. Put simply: God is the same as the universe. The universe is the same as me. And I am the same as God. A warmed-over version of Hinduism, New Age religion is completely self-centered and human-centered.

57

The obsession with angels has gone beyond biblical limits. The Bible never teaches us to pray to angels and ask for their guidance. Angels are sent by God, at God's initiative, to accomplish God's will in the way God wants — not in the way we want. The Bible clearly warns that we battle against evil angels — principalities and powers in the heavenly places, and demonic spirits. These are now promoted as good beings and objects of our prayer.

The earth is the Lord's, the Bible says. But New Age Spirituality wants us to think that the earth itself is God to be revered and worshipped. Pagan religion, so clearly denounced in the Old and New Testament, is now popular in North America.

There is a crisis of the soul because God and his revealed truth have been rejected by most of our universities. Our young people, raised in Christian homes and churches, are rapidly losing their faith in college. The results, as exemplified in the lives featured in Chapter Two, are profound, disastrous, and disturbing.

Crisis of the Heart. For thirty years now, the family has been systematically attacked by Western society. Now sexual perversion and homosexuality are openly taught, promoted, and encouraged in our universities and through the media. Freshmen in college are forced to watch homosexual videos in order to overcome their alleged "homophobia" (fear of homosexuals), often during orientation week before the first week of classes. Abuse of all sorts is the natural result of this degeneration of morals.

When the family is weak, people hurt. Since Sigmund Freud taught us to look at the human being in terms of unconscious drives, people are bringing their hurts out in the open. And they cry, "I hurt!" Like the young adults in Chapter Two, they may turn angry. Some are angry at the world; others are angry about their past. Millions of people need hope. Many have tried all kinds of therapy, and now therapy is in crisis. No wonder, when God's textbook for living is rejected, how can we change people's minds and hearts?

Crisis of the Will. There is a major crisis in North America concerning credibility. Leaders in church and government lack integrity. And we Christians lack the boldness to speak up for truth. And when Christians do speak up, they find themselves in a "culture war," being ridiculed because they dare to believe in a moral standard.

Young people more than ever need role models of holiness, righteousness, courage, loyalty, faithfulness, and diligence. These virtues take time, sacrifice, and persistence to develop. Such willpower is rare in our society today. Both adults and young people need strength in the soul in order to stand up for God's holy, righteous standards.

Time for Action

How shall the church of Jesus Christ face these crises? Some say that there have always been problems in a world without Christ. True enough. Historians are trained to detect similar trends across centuries. However, the proportions of the change going on around us today are mind-boggling, and our present crises calls for careful reflection and planned action:

Study Doctrine. The human mind, created by God, is hungry and thirsty for truth, absolute truth. We need to study the Bible in order to gain godly wisdom (Colossians 1:9-11). We must believe, when we study the Bible, that it contains a system (or body) of truths (or doctrines) which is practical for holy living. You and I may never gain a perfect and totally accurate understanding of that system of truths. But this does not change the fact that this system of truths exists in the Bible. If we give up believing that a body of truths exists in the Bible, we give up the possibility of knowing truth. We are then no better than our non-Christian postmodern contemporaries.

We should study the Bible to discover this system of truths. We should know it, believe in it, and depend on it to guide us through life. We should obey it, love it, proclaim it, and defend it against secular thought patterns. The core of this system of truths teaches that a personal and an absolute God exists. He created the world, and all men and women know God through his creation. Jesus Christ is God who came to the world to save sinners. Jesus died and rose again from the dead to overcome sin, death, and the devil. The Holy Spirit is a person who will empower all who are willing to be filled by him. There will be an end to history, and Jesus will personally return.

Christians need to know what they believe in. We begin with a careful, systematic study (not just casual reading) of the Bible.

Understand Contemporary Thought. Study the trends of thought being promoted in our world today. Go to a Christian bookstore, and buy a book on postmodernity. I recommend Stanley Grenz's *A Postmodernism Primer.* Or read Steve Garber's *Fabric of Faithfulness,* which challenges us to build truth and character into our young people, by being role models and fostering community with them. We need to teach them, but we also need to cry with them, and wipe our tears away, together.

Learn about the perverse teachings being spread in our schools today, even if it makes you sick. (For example: at Halloween, children learn that being a witch is fun. A very popular storybook tells how a girl has two lesbian mothers.) Remember: our children are learning these ideas in school. Learn so that we can be on guard.

Strengthen Teens. We need to equip our teenagers against the pagan ideas they will face in college. Teach them apologetics, ethics, literary and art criticism, and, social and political theory, from a Christian perspective. Remember: they will face these issues in college. Being admitted to our nation's finest higher institutions of learning is no guarantee that they will graduate as godly men and women. As a matter of fact, chances are they will imbibe some of postmodernism's worst ideas, unless the Spirit of God, by his grace, protects and teaches them. Solid training in how to defend the faith is essential.

The Chinese church has traditionally ignored the study of doctrine and apologetics. We are now reaping the fruit of decades of negligence and ignorance.

It is not too late. Parents, study what your children study. See how history books are rewritten to eliminate God from any role in history. Then tell your children about our Christian heritage (read some church history books and biographies, for example, *Great Leaders of the Christian Church; Church History in Plain Language; From Jerusalem to Irian Jaya; Escape From Reason; How Should We Then Live;* and so forth).

Be Open about Yourself. Parents, be open about your own weaknesses and injuries. Get help, and then tell your children about the mercy and grace of God in your lives.

When I was pastoring an English congregation in Chicago (1992-1995), my American-born Chinese members appreciated it when I talked about my weaknesses. They do not want a perfect pastor — they know that such does not exist! They want to know that I am struggling to love God, to obey him, and to serve him, and that I am making an effort and making progress, by God's grace. They want to see a slice of me, the real me, and not a false, plastic me.

Our young people are hungry and thirsty for role models who are honest with themselves, with God, and before others.

Prepare to Pay a Price. We need to be ready to suffer for our faith — this will come either to us or our children, but unless God revives the church to revive society (it is up to his sovereign will, in response to the prayers of his people), we are in for very difficult times as Christians. We will be ridiculed, harassed, and ostracized. The New Testament call to carry our cross may become a reality.

We in the West can learn a lot from Christians in China and other places where persecution is taking place right now. And these Christians are coming to North America in increasing numbers. Let us listen to them, humbly learn from them, and develop a spiritual alertness which the Apostle Peter prescribed (I Peter 5:8).

A final word: our young people are building relationships, and are encouraging and supporting each other in a world of turmoil. This is good and very important; it makes up for a real lack in their parents' generation. My prayer is that as they build relationships and practice encouragement, they do not throw truth out the window. Let truth govern their relationships. Let truth and love go hand in hand. And as they learn to obey the truth, they will surrender their wills to Christ, and become truly strong within.

God is a merciful God. He does not change. His faithfulness and his protection will always be with his people. We live in dangerous times. Let us lean on him and his promises — alone — for the road ahead. For we need Jesus badly — but we do have Jesus.

Summing Up The Past

In order to understand the complexities of the Chinese Christian community in North America, we must understand some of its history. People do not enter the world as autonomous spheres of existence, totally separated from the past. Even before we exit the womb, we are tossed into the swimming pool of common humanity; we partake in social, economic and cultural structures which were pre-established before our birth. These institutions influence us whether or not we want them to, and whether or not we know that they do.

Chinese-American Christians are no different. To varying degrees, all Chinese people have remnants of "Chinese-ness" within them. Some are saturated, while others only have two drops in them. At the same time, having lived in North America for however many years, all Chinese-Americans have assimilated to some degree into the Western mindset. Some of them have become "Twinkies" (that is, yellow on the outside, white on the inside), while others still feel alien to the American culture. Nevertheless, all have absorbed some American-ism through the inevitable process of cultural osmosis. Also, when a Chinese-American becomes a Christian and decides (or is forced) to attend a Chinese church, they wrap themselves in the historical blanket of the Chinese church and feed on its heritage. As a result, the Chinese-American Christian is a complex entity, a presentation of an eclectic inheritance of worldviews and values.

This section explores each of those three heritages that are collected in the Chinese-American Christian — Chinese history in China (Chapter Four) and overseas (Chapter Five), Western/American history (Chapter Six), and the history of the Chinese church in North America (Chapter Seven). In other words, this section will describe the making of a North-American Chinese Christian.

The Perplexities of
Chinese History and Culture:
The Road to Tiananmen Square and Beyond

We begin with insights from Chinese history and culture on our journey to explore the perplexities of the Chinese community in North America. We cannot ignore the past; the past continues to shape, limit and haunt us. The Holy Spirit will transform Chinese culture; but it does so as we face up to and own our past as ours, for what it is, and as we commit our past and "give them all to Jesus."

Culture and Politics as Identity:
From Culture to Politics, or Political Cultures?

What does it mean to be Chinese? What does "Chinese-ness" consist of? To put the question in the words of the philosopher Feng Yu-lan, what is the "spirit of Chinese philosophy?" As we contrast traditional and modern (post-Opium War) Chinese culture, we are prone to think that, whereas the traditional sense of Chinese-ness is a "cultural" one, the modern transformation consists of an evolution to a "political" sense of Chinese-ness. The traditional sense of being Chinese is that of being part of the universe under heaven (*tian xia*) in which the Emperor, the Son of Heaven, governs all classes — the scholar-gentry-official on the top, followed by the peasant, then the artisan, and finally the merchant. Each plays his or her role in society. The father is father to the son, the emperor is emperor to the official, the teacher is teacher to the student, and so forth; all are harmonious despite change. This sense of harmony amidst change was shattered with the impact of Western and Japanese aggression, beginning with the Opium War (1839-1842). China was rudely awakened to the fact that she was a nation in the modern, political sense of the term; and that as a nation, she was on the verge of extinction, almost going the route of Africa. How, then, should China "modernize" herself in order to maintain her dignity in the modern family of nations? Part of this "modernization" process — indeed, the very core of this process — consists of a transformed corporate understanding of what it means to be Chinese.

Having said this, one must immediately add that the traditional sense of Chinese-ness was not purely cultural, as if it were a-political. The Confucian ideal of harmony amidst change, and every person taking his or her place under heaven, was legitimized with the Legalist (*Fa jia*), authoritarian, political structure during the Chin and Han Dynasties (221 BC — 220 AD). Thus, Confucius' ethics were enforced with a penal system of imperial rule. Modern Maoist military and penal machines are, in one sense, only twentieth century versions of the Legalist rule. Therefore, politics have always been primary in Chinese society. Indeed, what we have witnessed in the past one hundred fifty years was the trading of one political culture (Confucianism-Legalism) for another (Communist Party-culture). A person is either on top or at the bottom, either an emperor or a peasant. There is precious little sense that all men and women are created equal with an equal sense of dignity.

Mysticism and Pragmatism:
Aesthetics and Ethics as the Spirit of Chinese Culture

In the mindset of the traditional Chinese scholar, literature and art play a much more significant role than in Western society. At the heart of the Confucian-Taoist worldview is a sense of mysticism — communion with nature, coupled with a pragmatic sense of ethics — being a moral example before the masses. Thus, the gentleman-scholar identifies with the sufferings of the people and the plight of the nation, and seeks to cultivate himself ethically and aesthetically in order to be of service to the nation. This is somewhat akin to the ideal of the Renaissance humanists (the teachers of rhetoric), who taught their students to speak eloquently as well as profoundly before the masses. We might note that neither the mystical element (communion with nature), nor the pragmatic-ethical element (being a moral example for the people), is particularly oriented to logic, cognition, analysis, or the scientific spirit. We might say that the traditional Confucian-Taoist worldview is right-brain-oriented.

When indigenous Chinese Christians, both liberal Protestant and fundamentalist evangelical, began to form their own theology in the 1920s, both wings of the Protestant church took a right-brain, mystical approach. Zhao Zichen (T.C. Chao), professor of theology at Yenching University, spoke of Jesus as the man who has attained the highest level of God-consciousness. Thus, He is our Savior, though a savior among many. One of Zhao's friends in the Suzhou-Shanghai area was philosopher N.Z. Zia (Xie Fu-ya). Zhao had the habit of drinking a bowl of warm salt water in the morning. On one occasion Zhao told Zia that he saw Jesus in the salt water (*zai yan tang li kan jian Ye su*)!

On the conservative side, we find Watchman Nee, as early as 1927, speaking of God's spirit being released when man's spirit is broken. Nee's trichotomy model of spirituality is highly mystical; he read about Christian mysticism while a college student in Fuzhou. Is there something intrinsically Chinese about this mystical approach? Is Chinese theology destined to become a "spiritual theology?"

I would like to propose that contemporary Chinese efforts to build a spiritual theology is very different from the aesthetics of the Confucian scholar. It is even different from Zhao's and Nee's mysticisms. Because of the onslaught of the modern world — industrialization, the profound is influenced by the technological. The mystic heart of Chinese culture is almost gone. Therefore, mysticism is an effort; it is a response to the technological world. Inasmuch as it is an answer, a therapy, or even a "way of escape," it is distinct and different from the mysticism which served as the heart and home of traditional Chinese culture. When the context changes, the heart of the culture changes its meaning as well. How does one teach prayer and meditation to urban Chinese young adults in Hong Kong, Toronto or Los Angeles? One books a gymnasium as a lecture hall; after the lectures, one sells the cassette tapes of the lectures. The context shapes the content; technology carries along the mysteries.

Identity: From Ethnocentrism to Crisis Consciousness

Beyond mysticism and pragmatism, a third theme in Chinese-ness emerges from modern Chinese intellectual history. It is the profound crisis in the Chinese consciousness that China, as a nation, was in deep trouble. Unless she adopts Western technology, she will be run over by the "barbarians" (Europeans) who have defeated her one battle after another. How should China modernize? Technology was the option attempted in the 1860s and 1870s, as China built arsenals, sent children abroad for study, and started a foreign language school for interpreters. By the 1890s, technology was not enough. Younger scholars proposed institutional changes to the throne — a constitutional monarchy. When the Empress Dowager suppressed the Hundred Days' Reform of 1898, the voice of reform was supplanted by the voice of revolution. The Manchu Dynasty was overthrown with the Revolution of 1911.

If technology, institutions and revolution were the proposals for modernization during the late nineteenth century, early twentieth century Chinese intellectuals saw a deeper crisis in Chinese culture. When the Confucian civil service examinations were abolished in 1905, the traditional means to preserve core values and the ladder of success in society were removed. By 1915, modern educated intellectuals (who still knew their Confucian classics) began to call for a "New Culture Movement" (*xin wen hua yun dong*). All of China's Confucian past must go; all of the Western culture (except Christianity and imperialism) should be adopted. This was the attitude of a number of Beijing University professors from 1915, up to the founding of the Chinese Communist Party in July 1921. Some of these intellectuals, the so-called "May Fourth" leaders, Christians among them, literally lost sleep because they saw that just because China had a constitution and a parliament, long-lasting change was not guaranteed unless a social consciousness, a "republican culture" (*gong he wen hua*) emerges among the people.

In twenty-eight years (1921-1949) the Chinese Communist Party evolved from an underground clique of Leninist intellectuals to the ruling party in China. Yet, as Chinese history seeks to move beyond the Tiananmen tragedy of June 4, 1989, the emerging theme among intellectuals is again a "crisis of consciousness." What does it mean to be Chinese? It means sharing a common memory of pain, anger, disillusionment, and dehumanization. We almost lost what it means to be human during the Cultural Revolution; many lost their sanity. The fabric of family life has been permanently transformed; with the one-child policy, four grandparents and two parents (usually) pour their attention and affection on one child. Gone are the days of deference, frugality and filial piety. As these children grow up, pain becomes even more of a reality for the parents, and for society at large.

How does one deal with this memory? One way is through hedonism and the pursuit of wealth, along with the spoiling of children. Let us vicariously enjoy the material things of life, or let the children do so, in a hurry! Another way to deal with the painful memory is through literature and the arts, social and economic research, and political action. Hope, for the Chinese, must find a way. This "crisis of consciousness" was the very stuff that made the May Fourth individuals who they were; it is also the very stuff that defines China's intellectuals today.

This Present Moment

What does it mean to be Chinese on the eve of the twenty-first century? It means one must face up to the "closed door." The theme from the motion picture, *The Last Emperor*, is pregnant with meaning. Every time the Chinese people (personified by the emperor) sought to go beyond the gate, the gate slammed shut. Is not this the same theme in the television series *River Elegy* (1988) — that the Great Wall was built not to keep the barbarians out, but to keep the Chinese in? What then? One looks within. What does one find within? A crisis of consciousness, "no exit."

All is not lost, however. This is not May 4, 1919 when the May Fourth era was inaugurated; this is June 4, 1989, and beyond. With telecommunications and concerned people around the world, Chinese intellectuals are rapidly joining the global community. We must learn, at every step of the way, what it means to be human and Chinese at the same time. Is this what time it is? Is this the present hour of Chinese consciousness? When we witness the outpouring of sentiment before and after June Fourth among overseas Chinese in North America, we can be sure that many share in this crisis of consciousness. During the long night, when people no longer march on the streets, we can know that we all share in our common search for hope.

One of the most important ways Christians can make a response to contemporary Chinese intellectuals is to share and to give a Christian answer to the question of suffering. Hope, after all, lies not in the fax machine, nor in the United Nations, but ultimately in Jesus Christ.

The Perplexities of
Overseas Chinese Communities:
The Road to Chinatown

Overseas Chinese Communities in Southeast Asia

In traditional China, it was illegal to emigrate outside the Empire. However, because of natural disasters, famine, wars, and population explosion, Chinese emigration increased significantly in the nineteenth century. From the coastal provinces of Fujian and Guangdong, Chinese people moved to Southeast Asian countries where they prospered through hard work. Politically, they were often discriminated against and occasionally persecuted by their host country (among the host countries are Malaysia and Indonesia); but they continued to live and work, largely in silence. They built Chinese language schools for their children to preserve the Chinese culture. Theirs was a long-distance, nostalgic identification with Chinese culture; in leaving China, they became more Chinese.

In the 1970s and 1980s, however, three trends significantly transformed the profile of this overseas Chinese community. First, the Vietnam War and its aftermath brought thousands of ethnic Chinese refugees (many were among the "boat people") to a life of exile, many of them immigrating to the West. The painful memories of the "killing fields" of Indochina will continue to impact a whole generation as they seek to resettle, to forget and to press on.

Second, the economic miracle of the Little Dragons of East Asia (South Korea, Taiwan, Hong Kong, and Singapore) has transformed many overseas Chinese into sophisticated, urban Asians with a global perspective and lifestyle. Business people and artists travel from Asia to Europe and North America regularly. Hong Kong became the world's third largest gold market and the world's second largest container port. Japan and Taiwan held the world's largest and second largest cash reserves respectively. Singapore boasts the world's best airport recognized by the international travel industry.

Third, such accomplishments meant that while the West came to the East (whether in the form of missionaries or Western students of Buddhism and Hinduism in Asia), the East moved on toward the modern West, or more accurately, to a global consciousness. The children of overseas Chinese (for example, Singaporeans and Indonesian Chinese) are forging an international intercultural identity with it own unique dynamics, increasingly drawing attention in the West, but seldom understood. In the Christian community, the Indonesian-speaking Chinese churches are more in number and larger in size than the Chinese-speaking churches. In Singapore, English-speaking churches are more in number and larger in size than Chinese-speaking Chinese churches. "Chinese-ness" is on the move!

Where does this "globalization" bring us? It carries us to the same point that the development of Western civilization brings us: to a crisis of human values. Memories, whether of the Cultural Revolution in China, or eyewitnesses to the Vietnam War, are real and painful. Spoiled children from mainland China and prosperous ethnic Chinese Singaporeans have not experienced hunger and poverty. We are approaching a period in history in which the traditional values of Confucianism (and perhaps of Christianity as well) will be more a memory than a reality. New

Confucianism is trying very hard to demonstrate the relevance of Confucian values for the postmodern age. Christian education, and education in general, will become more challenging.

This is the context for understanding the Chinese community in North America. We limit our understanding if we look at the American-born Chinese (ABCs) in isolation from the global Chinese community.

Overseas Chinese Communities in North America

American interests in nineteenth century China followed British patterns: after the Opium War (1839-1842) and the Nanjing Treaty (1842), the Americans negotiated parallel treaties with China (1843-1844) in which the right of extraterritoriality was granted to Western nations. This right allowed non-Chinese expatriates to be tried by the laws of their home country, in a non-Chinese court on Chinese soil.

During the 1840s Chinese people immigrated to North America in search of gold. After the gold rush they worked on building America's transcontinental railroads. During this period, the United States Congress passed the Exclusionary Act (1882) which barred Chinese families from being united in America. The Exclusionary Act only applied to Chinese, and was not repealed until 1943, the year in which the privilege of extraterritoriality in the unequal treaties was also abolished.

Since 1945 several waves of Chinese immigration to the United States can be discerned. During the Korean War the U.S. State Department required Chinese students to remain in America; they were given aid to complete their education. This generation has since largely assimilated into American society, and comprise the elite circles of Chinese society in North America.

In the 1960s, relaxed immigration laws brought a new wave of immigrants to North America. During this period foreign students began to come to North America to study in large numbers. They came from Taiwan and Hong Kong, with a smaller number from Southeast Asia. Many of them (over 90% of students from Taiwan) remained in America after graduation, and raised their families here. Christians among this group started hundreds of Chinese churches in the 1970s and 1980s.

The United States withdrew from Vietnam in 1975 and recognized China in 1979. These events brought new waves of Chinese immigration: refugees from Indochina; exchange scholars and students from mainland China; and immigrants from the People's Republic of China coming to reunite with their families in North America. Many of the visa students (and some of the immigrants) coming from urban Hong Kong and Taipei are more affluent and more sophisticated in outlook than the previous generation. This makes the Chinese community in North America extremely diverse and complex.

Parallel to each wave of immigration is a period of second-generation ABCs. They are the children of the Korean War-period students, and are mature adults today. The children of the students of the 1960s and 1970s are in college and the workplace; there they are meeting other children of the immigrants of the 1960s and 1970s. They are seeking to make their presence felt in American society, although their identity as Asian-Americans seems to be in transition, moving towards mainstream American culture. Whereas the second-generation ABCs of the 1960s (children of an earlier, secluded Chinese community) tend to reject Chinese culture, in the 1990s an increasing proportion of Chinese-American young adults tend to affirm certain aspects of Chinese culture with confidence and pride, while embracing the lifestyle of their host countries, the United States and Canada. (The author does recognize that a number of Chinese-American young adults are also growing up in Mexico today. But since this phenomenon is still small compared to the influx of Chinese people in Canada and in the United States, we will limit our observations of North America to the United States and Canada only.) They tend to be what sociologists Dan Sue and Gerald Sue call "traditionalist" Chinese-Americans (for more on this refer to Chapter Eight). The Civil Rights movement in the United States, the subsequent affirmation of ethnic identity by Americans, and Canada's and the United States' recognition of the People's Republic of China, certainly contributed to this change. Thus, there is a higher degree of assimilation into American society, and at the same time a higher level of identification with the Chinese community.

Among first-generation immigrants and second- and third-generation ABCs, we detect a continuum (or spectrum) of individuality and tastes. An individual immigrant may be more Chinese (traditional) or more American (assimilated) than another individual, or they may be in the process of assimilating. An ABC individual may identify more with Chinese culture or with American culture, or they may be caught in between, reacting against and rejecting certain aspects from both cultures.

Such a spectrum may be construed to refer to individuals, or traits within an individual. For example, an individual may be very American when it comes to recreation, but very Chinese in tastes for food; very American when it comes to management style at the workplace, but very Chinese in leadership style (or expectations of leadership) at home, at church, and in the Chinese community.

East is meeting West in Asia, and both are caught in the crosscurrents; the Chinese community in North America is a microcosm of this. Diversity, movement and change characterize the Chinese identity. Does this pose a threat to the immigrant's search for security when we discover that "Chinese-ness" is a very elusive thing? Self-understanding is never easy, but when the very dimensions of the task are denied by an individual, it becomes both difficult and threatening. Whether one recognizes the crosscurrents or denies it, we are all caught up in a crisis of consciousness.

The Search for Community

What will tomorrow's Chinese community look like? While in selected areas we are making great achievements, it seems that in other areas the Chinese community will need to step up her involvement in the North American context. Indications are that she has begun to do so.

First, Chinese parents need to encourage their children to be involved and to achieve in the fields of the humanities and social sciences. The development of significant ideas which contribute to a society's worldview often takes place in these fields, although science plays an important part as well. There are reasons why this has not been the case, and they stem from the Chinese background, as well as from the Christian background. Somewhere in the painful modern transformation, the mystical aspect of the Chinese worldview was relegated to the background, while the pragmatic or moral aspect was transformed to a flexible, but often opportunistic instinct for survival. The humanities are not good business; medicine, business and technology are. The fundamentalist aversion to fully participate in society, thought and culture (partly for fear that we would lose our faith in the process) further discourages Chinese youth from going into the humanistic and social science disciplines.

Second, Chinese youth need to be encouraged to enter the

political arena and fully participate in the democratic process in North America. Their one hundred fifty-year search for nationhood notwithstanding, overseas Chinese people continue to sustain an "I-it" relationship to the state. This is particularly true among the unregistered or house churches in China. Fundamentalist Christianity discourages Christians from participating in politics. What this often means is an implicit approval and support of the existing regime. However, new developments are pushing Christians into the political arena, among them the Taiwanese, mainland Chinese students overseas, and (since the 1980s) Hong Kong Chinese.

Third, Chinese people need to develop a generous sacrificial spirit of philanthropy. Christians need to demonstrate this spirit of civic involvement beyond the four walls of the church. Volunteer non-profit organizations are an integral part of a civil society. Christian concepts of tithing and faith-promise offerings may be extended to the community at large through example and consciousness-raising.

What we have seen is the need to fulfill the ideals of Confucianism, a return to the world of letters and ideas, and to the world of politics through setting a civic example. Do these needs point to the demise of Confucianism? Do these point to ways in which Christianity can fulfill the highest aspirations of Confucianism by supplying the dynamic lacking in Confucian humanism?

Fourth, Chinese people need to develop a true sense of appreciation of foreign cultures (including minority cultures in China). We need to be truly global and cross-cultural, not only through our immigration patterns, our travel, and our ability to be adaptable in foreign cultures, but through building personal and institutional relationships based on trust, dignity, equality, appreciation, and mutual empowerment. Here is where Confucianism and Chinese ethnocentric pride needs to be disciplined and supplanted by the Christian spirit of mission and the concept of the unity of the Body of Christ. And in this search for mission and unity, we meet the American-born Chinese Generation X, for he or she, too, is hungry for community.

Conclusion

The Chinese individual is at a crossroads today. Whether as an immigrant to North America or as a second- or third-generation ABC, the individual carries the baggage of Chinese and Western values and beliefs all mixed up into one concoction. A "crisis of consciousness" develops as the individual seeks for his or her own special identity. In part this will be fulfilled as the Chinese community in North America accepts and embraces this individual into the family. And what the individual will look like will be determined by the Chinese community's involvement in the context of North American society and culture. East is indeed meeting West; where will the Chinese community exist within this convergence?

The Perplexities of American Society and Culture:
The Road to Postmodernity

We have seen, in the last two chapters, how the roots of the contemporary Chinese community in North America lie deep in Chinese history and in the history of Chinese immigration. North American society, however, has been shaped in its cultural expression by modern Western thought as well as by the Christian church. Therefore, we live in the context that is North America, and the sojourning experience of the Chinese community in North America has profoundly impacted the Chinese mind. It is to these dynamics that we now turn to in our search for an understanding of the Chinese community in North America.

The Crisis of Modern Western Thought

Two parallel developments in the history of Western thought shape the contemporary West. One originates from Greek philosophy, finding modern expression in the Renaissance and continuing to develop through the Enlightenment, all the way up to Immanuel Kant and nineteenth century thought. The other begins from the Old and New Testaments, and develops through the Protestant Reformation, the Great Awakening, and up to twentieth century American evangelicalism.

In the sixteenth and seventeenth centuries science and philosophy sought to "liberate" themselves from the shackles of the church. In so doing, they established humankind as the autonomous judge of all reality. Seventeenth century rationalism set up the human mind as the autonomous arbiter of truth. Eighteenth century empiricism and skepticism offered the human senses of perception as the independent judge of facts. Immanuel Kant summed up this modern enlightenment project by dividing the universe into two realms: (1) the *phenomenal realm*, in which the laws of logic and science operate, and (2) the *noumenal realm*, in which religious and ethical principles (that is, love) govern deliberations. Kant sought to do justice to the need for rigorous logical and scientific thinking, on the one hand, and the universal human need to ground morality in some absolute principle, on the other hand. In separating the noumenal realm from the realm of logic and science, Kant made religion and ethics subjective rather than objective realities. God is a God of love, but he no longer informs us with facts in history and science.

Nineteenth century thought followed Kant in embracing subjectivity as a norm. Friedrich Schleiermacher saw the essence of religion not so much in objective divine revelation, but in the subjective human feeling of absolute dependence on some infinite force in the universe (which he variously called God or nature). Materialism followed Schleiermacher in the thought of Ludwig Feuerbach, who substituted a human-centered religion in the modern world for the outdated God-centered religion in the primitive world. Karl Marx simply turned Feuerbach economic and developed his dialectical materialism and utopian dream for a communist society.

Subjectivity found further expression in nineteenth century existentialism through Soren Kierkegaard, whose concern was first and foremost the here and the now, the moment in which human beings face their own predicament. Karl Barth, the twentieth century's first major Protestant theologian, followed Kierkegaard's approach to reality by asserting that God's Word can be understood primarily in the here and now as an existential event, rather than as objective propositions. If there is no objective truth in the universe, and there is no propositional truth given by God, all God-talk could only be studied linguistically and sociologically. Thus, the story of twentieth century philosophy and the sociology of knowledge was a study of the relation between the human mind, language and society, and culture. And for those who took this subjectivity to its logical conclusion, one determined that the universe is absurd and meaningless (for example, Jean-Paul Sartre and Albert Camus), or it is nothing but a collage of myths and ideologies. Postmodernist deconstructionism simply drew the conclusion that all words, being arbitrarily assigned as symbols, are meaningless.

The significance of all these developments in Western thought lies in the fact that modern methodologies, including the discipline of the sociology of knowledge (so-called "hermeneutics," not to be confused with the principles of grammatico-historical hermeneutics taught in the historic evangelical schools of theology, although the former is beginning to impact the latter), continues to exert a great influence upon young Chinese scholars, both Christian and secular. We breathe its air, we play according to its rules, and we employ its vocabulary. Even our understanding of traditional Chinese thought and culture is governed by the principles of the modern method.

When objectivity is eliminated from any quest for truth, the postmodern view that words have no meaning, history has no facts, and there is no right and wrong in ethics, is the only logical conclusion.

The Crisis of American Society

This secularization of the principle of certainty in knowledge greatly influences the development of Christianity in America. At the same time as, but distinct from, the Renaissance humanism in the sixteenth century, Martin Luther and John Calvin rediscovered the gospel and the Bible as the material and the formal principles for certainty in religious knowledge. Puritanism, a seventeenth century expression of Calvinism, took the doctrines of the gospel one step further in seeking to build a covenant community both in the church and in society. When England stifled the Puritan vision, immigrants found virgin soil in the American colonies to build a "city on a hill" in the 1620s and 1630s. If God has chosen to bind himself to the promises of the covenant of grace given to his elect people, then Christians are to bind themselves together as God's people — first as church, and then as society. When Christians live out the gospel as a nation, the world will stand up and take notice of their "good works" and give glory to the Father.

The Puritan plan for a Christian society had declined greatly by the early eighteenth century. The Great Awakening of the 1730s and 1740s rekindled the flame through preaching repentance to the church and through the establishment of Christian institutions of higher education throughout the colonies. Jonathan Edwards, preacher, historian of the revival, theologian, and philosopher, responded to the skepticism of his day by developing the Calvinist principles and applying it to human experience, especially the soul's experience of regeneration.

Evangelical Protestant response to secular Western thought, however, became passive by the nineteenth century. After the American Civil War (1861-1865), evangelicals abandoned the city, leaving it largely to liberal church leaders to evangelize the masses. Charles Darwin's evolution and historical criticism began to influence the theology of American seminaries by the 1880s. By the 1920s fundamentalists were on the defensive. Gresham Machen was ousted from the Presbyterian Church, USA in 1936. After World War II, evangelical leaders such as Carl Henry and Harold Lindsell, seeing the demise of Western civilization and the need for a Christian response, began to re-enter the world of thought and culture in order to establish a biblical witness there. Evangelicals have been striving in this direction for merely forty years, and we have a long way to go. As evangelicals grew in both number and influence, mainline churches, historically the depository of liberal theology for a century, faced a decline in her ranks in the past forty years. And this is where Generation X finds the evangelical church today.

In the past thirty years we witnessed the almost complete breakdown of historic Western civilization in North America. The counter-culture of the 1960s, and the quest for the good life of the 1980s, were both deliberate rebellious reactions against both Christianity and traditional values of family and civilization. Add to that the American sense of confusion and frustration as a result of the Vietnam War and the Watergate affair of the 1970s, and America was definitely "No. 2" (economically and in other ways) by the beginning of the Persian Gulf War of 1990-1991, despite her victory in the Cold War. Japan and Germany had overtaken America in key industries while American education is in deep trouble. One may conclude that not only the American mind, but also the American heart and will, are all closed, waiting to be re-opened by a new synthesis of culture, a new vision to re-construct Western, indeed, global civilization.

The American Church in Context

This is the critical situation in which the North American

85

church finds herself. The Puritans came to America to Christianize the land; evangelicals today need to hold on to this position, take the offensive, and re-Christianize America. Movements to restore the American family and humanity's role in it, and to address the needs of crisis pregnancies, can be understood in this light. Historically, the American church was the largest sending church in foreign missions. Today, many of the traditional mission fields — China, India, and the nations of Africa — are represented by immigrants on North American soil; furthermore, churches like those in China and Korea are taking the lead in spiritual power, church growth and world missions. The North American church finds herself no longer a unilateral sender, but a partner and increasingly a recipient in world evangelization as the message of the gospel is sent from all six continents to all six continents. Traditional evangelicals, deeply entrenched in a rural-oriented culture in the heartland of America, are still sorting out what all this means.

How does one operate in a world community in which no single culture dominates? How does one overcome the cultural blind-spots of yesteryear (that is, the imperialism of the Victorian era and the triumphalism of World War II and the Cold War) without wallowing in guilt in the face of the post-colonial resurgence of the Christian church in the Two-Thirds World, and without relativizing the absolute claims of the gospel? How can the Two-Thirds World Christians and ethnic Christians in North America relate to the predominantly Caucasian church on the basis of equality, dignity and a common call to servanthood, without unrighteous anger and a sense of revenge?

Dialogue in the post-colonial period is threatening; it is hard work. It involves facing racism and working to overcome it with grace and with boldness. This may bring disillusion to Generation Xers. But it is absolutely critical.

Chinese Community in American Context

If there is one thing that has characterized the Chinese community in North America since the early days of the gold rush, it is hard work. How do we explain this phenomenon? Work is the way to survival when pressures inside China propelled people to emigrate to Southeast Asia and North America. Second, the deep sense of humiliation and defeat that China experienced in the late nineteenth and early twentieth century was coupled with an urge to restore the glory of the Han people. There is a great deal to be done before China can be proud again; and the Chinese people have often been willing to sacrifice and work hard to recover this pride.

Traditionally, this hard work was done in isolation from mainstream American society as Chinese operated laundries and restaurants. As the second-generation grew up, coupled with the more recent immigrant waves since the mid-1960s, Chinese in North America are better equipped to directly compete in various fields in a multi-ethnic society. This is already accomplished in areas such as architecture (I.M. Pei), sports (Michael Chang), and computers (Wang An). The Massachusetts Institute of Technology (M.I.T.) was so fascinated by why Asians excelled in mathematics that more than once a research project was conducted on that question.

In a secular society competition is toward an end, the goal very often being financial reward and its corollaries (status, comfort, and so forth). Without the God of the Bible at the core of civilization, however, these can become substitutes for God. Thus, in the success which Chinese have enjoyed in selected areas of competition, we have participated in idol worship, while fooling ourselves to believe that all we are doing is participating in the so-called "Protestant" work ethic. We are better at this idol worship than our Caucasian contemporaries. We have a greater sense to achieve and restore our glory. But much of hard work is idol worship, unfortunately.

Hard work as idol worship is not the only way in which the Chinese have assimilated into American culture. The traditional emphasis on the Chinese family is eroding. Perhaps the traditional Chinese family was a myth, at a time when the head of the family held nominal power and control over all clan members. Unless we emulate and worship the God of the Bible — God, our Father — no human father, mother, or head of household can truly set a moral example and develop his or her family to its full potential. Today both American and Chinese families are being undermined as the secularization of society approaches its completion. At the same time, educational standards and expectations are going down — both among Americans and in significant sectors of the Chinese community. Academic performance, like wealth, is becoming polarized, with a few at the very top and more at the bottom.

Taipei, Hong Kong, and increasingly Shanghai, Guangzhou, and Beijing, are affluent cities. In the marketplace commerce is an art. True leadership involves integrity; but in the marketplace, the rules of the game are more often deceit than honesty. The Chinese community is not only eroding at the family level; ethical and moral integrity is also at risk. We, as an ethnic group, are in search of true leadership to guide us into the twenty-first century. Without true leadership, Generation X will continue in its pessimism and skepticism.

The Perplexities of Chinese Christian Communities in North America:
The Road to Churchhood

The Missionary Tradition

The Chinese church bears a twofold relationship with the Chinese community: on the one hand, the church wants to impact the community with the gospel; on the other hand, the church historically has been largely isolated from the community. What are the historical roots for this dual relationship?

The claims of the gospel do not change, but the forms of expressing the gospel change with time and vary from society to society. In order to understand the Chinese church's form of expressing the gospel, it is helpful to look at two revival movements in church history.

The Great Awakening that took place in the 1740s in the American colonies signified a model of revival that stressed both the repentance from sin and the building of the Christian mind. For preachers and teachers such as Theodore Jacobus Frelinghuysen, Jonathan Edwards, George Whitefield, and Gilbert and William Tennent, there was no dichotomy between a knowledge of God through the doctrines taught in the Bible, and a personal experience of God. There was a genuine concern to promote both a spirit of repentance, and a learned clergy and laity (see the Introduction of this book).

By the 1860s, however, another revival was to make such a dichotomy. Through the preaching of Dwight Moody, this revival was distinctly anti-intellectual; it was a reaction to liberal theology and the secularization of the mainline Protestant denominations. The result was that the Chinese church inherited, through the thousands of missionaries from North America (the number of Protestant missionaries working in China peaked at eight thousand in 1926), a version of evangelical piety which pitted the intellect against the spirit. The building up of the Christian mind was clearly missing in this revival (see Introduction).

Part of this evangelical fundamentalist anti-intellectualism was an aversion to the affairs of "secular" society, thought and culture. Jesus was to return soon, and thus, the church's main focus was to rescue individual souls from the dominion of the devil into the safe haven of the church. Gone were the twin emphases of the Great Awakening — *repentance* leading to a *renewal* of the Christian mind.

Most of the American missionaries who went to China came from the post-revolutionary, nineteenth century rural context of the American heartland. In the small community there was a down-home atmosphere, an emphasis on relationships, and a common man attitude which was suspicious of the intellectual elite of the East Coast. From these small towns and villages, missionaries went to a mission field which was very strange to them: the pre-revolutionary rural context of the Chinese hinterland. There a xenophobic gentry-scholar-official looked upon these foreign "barbarians" as intruders; missionary enterprises in education, relief and social reform were treated as efforts to supplant the gentry-scholar's social function on the local village level. The result was that by the 1860s there was a strong anti-missionary, anti-foreign tradition in China, with afterschock waves leading to the present day. The Christian church could not help but isolate herself from her opponents.

The anti-intellectual tradition, as well as the isolated position of the church in China, reinforced one another. In America, the anti-intellectual, anti-cultural stance began to change by the late 1940s, as Harold Ockenga, Charles Fuller, Carl Henry, Harold Lindsell, and others started Fuller Theological Seminary in 1948. In Philadelphia, theologian Cornelius Van Til was working out his presuppositional apologetics and writing a critique of the theology of Karl Barth in his book, *Christianity and Barthianism*. In the 1960s Francis Schaeffer and others sought to speak the historic Christian faith to the twentieth century generation of hippies. In the 1990s, Charles Colson, Mortimer Adler, Ravi Zacharias, and Os Guinness continue this tradition of penetrating the halls of politics, culture and the arts with the gospel. The Chinese church, however, has a long way to go before she catches up to share this new vision of interacting with and penetrating contemporary culture.

The Chinese Christian Tradition

While the Chinese church inherited an anti-intellectual tradition, her ranks began to be filled with intellectuals in the twentieth century. This was to become increasingly problematic: how can Chinese intellectuals be discipled to impact culture without being secularized by the culture in the process?

Not all of the missionaries who went to China were anti-intellectual. The mainline denominations, in particular, were starting colleges and universities by the 1880s. In the first half of the twentieth century, there were over a dozen Protestant universities in China, such as Yenching in Beijing, Cheeloo in Shangtung, St. John's in Shanghai, Soochow University, and Lingnan in Guangzhou. The graduates of these universities went on to fulfill their parents' aspirations: they entered the business or other professional fields. Many of them came to North America. When the Korean War broke out the United States government required them to stay, and gave them financial aid to complete their education. These graduates became the first generation of Chinese professionals in North America. Having received a liberal Protestant education, they were now largely secularized.

In the 1960s and 1970s Chinese students began coming to North America to further their studies. The Christians among them started Bible study groups and Christian fellowships, which were largely independent and unaffiliated with any denomination or student movement (for example, InterVarsity, Campus Crusade, and The Navigators). This independence was borrowed from the fundamentalist spirituality of the church in China, Taiwan and Hong Kong. In addition to being anti-intellectual, isolated, and alienated from the organized church, a sense of belonging to the local congregation as full-fledged members was conspicuously missing among most Chinese Christian students. This trend is somewhat changing in the 1980s and 1990s as these same students started their own congregations (mostly independent in polity) and became leaders in them.

These developments mean that the identity and spirituality of the Chinese church in North American are often defined and perceived in isolation both from the secular culture of the Chinese community and the overall North American context. And within the Chinese Christian community the student Bible study groups continue to develop independently of the Chinese churches (although in some cases, some Chinese churches worked to "absorb" these groups as college-age fellowships within their congregations).

The Metamorphosis of the Chinese Church in North America

The development of the Chinese church in North America during the second half of the twentieth century can be thought of in three phases:

The Shaping of a Community (1943-1963)

1943 may seem to be a year of little significance in world history, but three momentous developments changed the place of the Chinese people in the world. First of all, the Chinese Exclusionary Act passed by the United States Congress in 1882 was finally repealed. The Chinese, who had the "honor" of being the only foreign race formally excluded from immigration to the United States, were now free to bring over their wives and families. Chinese-American families began to grow in North America. In addition, the principle of "extraterritoriality" was terminated, allowing China to try foreigners who reside in China, in Chinese courts according to Chinese law. Finally, China, now an equal partner in the world of nation-states, fully participated in World War II as one of the Allies.

When the war was over, China plunged into four years of weary civil war. The Chinese Communist Party proclaimed the birth of the People's Republic in 1949; soon thereafter the United States entered the Korean War. In the mid-1950s, the McCarthyist fear gripped the American people, and many were suspected to be Communist spies in America. Around 1960 the United States, spurred by the Sputnik incident, committed herself to the arms and space race. Scientists and engineers became the people of the hour to help the United States develop into a world power.

Along with the surge of science and technology, the standard of living rose as well. The refrigerator, the family car, color television, and home appliances of all sorts began to infiltrate every American home in the 1950s. This period is what Clarence Cheuk calls the "Silent Generation" (see Chapter One). In this context of technological progress and materialistic lifestyle, the Chinese began to emigrate to America in increasing numbers. Although immigration in this period cannot compare with the later floodtide of the 1960s and 1970s, it was still truly a beginning. Especially with the immigration of Chinese women, children were born — the American-born Chinese. Furthermore, with the Korean War going on, Chinese-Americans were given scholarships to complete their studies, and many went on to become doctors, diplomats and other professionals. A two-part Chinese community thus took shape: immigrant and student, worker and professional, urban and suburban, struggling and successful. The Chinese community began to take shape.

During this period the mainline Protestant denominations in North America continued their long-established pattern of supporting home missions work among the Chinese in large cities — San Francisco, Los Angeles, Chicago, New York, Philadelphia, and so forth. Evangelical churches also sent lay (mostly female) workers to start Sunday School classes among Chinese children, and English and Bible classes among Chinese women.

Among the students, many began to come together for fellowship and Bible study. In 1957 a summer conference was held at York, Pennsylvania, drawing one hundred students. From this conference *Ambassadors* magazine was launched. This magazine was later published by Ambassadors for Christ, an organization which started in Washington D.C. in 1963. In 1961, Thomas Wang started Chinese Christian Mission, a ministry of mass evangelism, in a backyard garage in Detroit, Michigan. Other evangelists, such as Moses Yu and Calvin Chao, started student ministries (often with hostel facilities), which soon developed into churches. The pattern of para-church organizations, serving the Chinese church and planting new ones, was now set.

Much of evangelism and discipleship followed established evangelical patterns of the church in China and Asia. Students and immigrants, often experiencing "culture shock" (although the term may not have been coined yet) in a foreign land, responded to the gospel of Jesus Christ and grew in their personal relationship with their Savior. Their piety and zeal were nurtured by the local church and student fellowship. This provided a foundation upon which later ministries were to build from.

The Death of Christian Civilization and the Institutionalization of the Chinese Church (1963-1979)

Things began to move with amazing speed in the 1960s, leaving many people in bewilderment, helplessness and "rootlessness." Early in this decade, the Beatles made their debut in Liverpool, England, launching the Rock'n'Roll era. The Free Speech Movement in Berkeley, California soon spread to most major campuses in North America. Students, protesting against the Vietnam War and the evils of capitalistic society, occupied the library of Columbia University in 1968, confronted the police at Kent State University, Ohio in 1971, and escaped into sex and drugs in the name of "making love, not war."

The antiwar movement did make a significant impact upon American society. Besides the Vietnam War, the Watergate scandal (1972-1974) completed the process of undermining Americans' confidence in any type of politics. Problems with energy (beginning with the oil crisis in the mid-1970s), the environment, and the economy drove many Americans to pursue personal financial security. In this mood of pessimism, some Americans — including mission and denominational leaders — looked to the

Marxist countries, especially the People's Republic of China, as an alternative model for developing a new humanity and society. Since information coming out of China was scarce, these Christian leaders idealized the Cultural Revolution into a twentieth century exodus. Mao Zedong was the new Moses; salvation in Jesus Christ was replaced by the emergence of the Socialist Man. Evangelicals, led by David Adeney, continued to pray that China's doors to the gospel might open one day.

Traditional Christian civilization, along with values which emphasize the dignity of humanity and the importance of family and community, crumbled before our eyes. Divorce became commonplace; abortion was easily accessible; homosexuals, women, and other minorities began to clamor for their rights. The gospel soon came under fire.

Into this scene came the Chinese, immigrating to America by the thousands following the Kennedy Act (1965), which increased the quota of immigrants from countries outside the Western Hemisphere. Families, workers and students poured into America's cities. Some of these students protested in 1971 when Japan took over the Tiao-yu-t'ai Islands at the moment when Okinawa returned to Japanese control. A brief student movement came on the scene in the early 1970s, but soon splintered into several factions — pro-Chiang Kai-shek, pro-Taiwanese independence, pro-mainland, pro-Asian-American, and others. Meanwhile, the children of the Korean War generation of Chinese students grew up, and a whole breed of American-born Chinese young adults permanently changed the profile of the Chinese community.

Among the immigrants and students who came in the 1960s and 1970s were Christian families, students and ministers. The students spontaneously formed their own Chinese Bible study groups (CBSGs) or Chinese Christian Fellowships (CCFs). This was a unique phenomenon among all the foreign students in North America during this period; no other group of foreign students formed as many spontaneous, student-run and independent Christian fellowships as the Chinese.

Many of these groups came together for regional summer/winter conferences but never approached a continent-wide congress (though many were dreaming of such an ideal and exploring strategy and direction for the student movement). Some of the student groups began to experiment with inductive Bible study, a method made popular by InterVarsity Christian Fellowship, but which originated at the New York Biblical Seminary in the early 1950s. This technique took the methods of literary analysis and applied it to the Bible (this was referred to by Natalie Leong in Chapter Two). Although not every Chinese Bible study group adopted this method, it became widely used in many regions, beginning in the West Coast through the efforts of a small group of leaders at the University of California, Berkeley.

Along with inductive Bible study came mass communications. The Berkeley Chinese Christian Fellowship produced *Metamorphosis II*, a slide/sound production depicting the plight of the Chinese student in America, and presenting the gospel in the context of friendship evangelism and the outreach of the Chinese Christian Fellowship. The slide-sound combination became very popular throughout the 1970s; not only were presentations made for evangelism, but many Christian organizations began using this technique for promotion and fundraising.

Christian students were trained in a variety of skills and used many of these skills for their evangelistic outreach and discipleship. Many students, some of whom later became professors and scientists, critiqued evolution from a creationist point of view. Others translated significant evangelical books from

97

English into Chinese. Still others used their financial resources, either for grants to those ministries in need (including seminary students, such as The Seminary Scholarship Fund Committee), or for investments made for profit-making enterprises (the profits were then used for evangelistic or evangelical causes, such as Organization, Management and Finance, Inc. [OMFI]).

A very significant development in all of this was the adoption of marketing techniques, both in mass communication (audience research), and in itinerating and promotion. Christian organizations began to promote their ministries in North America, using slide-sound presentations, setting up regional committees or boards, and issuing news bulletins. The Chinese church in North America became institutionalized.

In this context of rapid social change, and with the adoption of secular techniques of communications and marketing in ministry, Chinese churches began to be planted in great numbers. Many graduates from universities and graduate schools started their own churches; some of these churches were little more than extensions of existing student-run CBSGs or CCFs. Other congregations were started because of interpersonal communication breakdowns and power struggles; these churches comprised a very significant proportion of the total of Chinese churches in North America. Immigrant churches, along with Chinatown-bred American-born Chinese young adults, grew in number. The numerical growth of suburban-bred, American-raised Chinese had just begun; they were destined to enter prestigious schools and become influential and successful in their career fields. This latter group, the suburban American-born or American-raised Chinese, would become very significant in the 1990s, as they began to drop out of church after entering college (as Chapter Two amply demonstrates).

Along with the growth of both immigrant and student/professional churches came immigrant pastors and their families. They, like their laypeople, came under tremendous "culture shock," but sought to adjust and survive in a rapidly changing society. (Those who immigrated in the 1980s and 1990s seem to have less difficulties in adjustment, having lived through Taipei's and Hong Kong's transition to global cities.) They brought over Asian models of church ministry, and ministered most effectively to Asian-bred, Chinese-speaking believers. Many of the hot issues posed by the 1960s and 1970s were bypassed by many Chinese churches (while their counterparts in Taiwan and Hong Kong began to face these social issues with great honesty and courage), although there was a small minority who cried out for change.

With the increasing number of Chinese churches and student groups, a sense of solidarity grew. Many Chinese students attended Urbana, InterVarsity's triennial missionary convention held at the University of Illinois, and with them came student workers and pastors. Some of these pastors gathered at Urbana 1970 and planned the North America Congress of Chinese Evangelicals (NACOCE), which was held in December 1972. The West Coast Chinese Christian Students Winter Conference cancelled their 1972 conference and contributed local manpower toward NACOCE's on-site operation. NACOCE was held subsequently at Wheaton, Illinois (1974), Toronto, Canada (1978), Pasadena, California (1979), and Chicago (1983). After 1986, NACOCE was renamed Chinese Coordination Centre of World Evangelism-North America (CCCOWE-NA). Today it is known as two entitites: CCCOWE-USA and CCCOWE-Canada.

Many Christians became enthusiastic about the vision of greater cooperation and unity, and came to befriend believers and church leaders from various regions of North America. At

NACOCE 1972, the faculty-in-preparation of China Graduate School of Theology (which opened in Hong Kong in 1975) and leaders of China Evangelical Seminary (which opened in Taipei in 1970) discussed the possibility of a merger. At NACOCE 1978 in Toronto, four American-born Chinese pastors (Hoover Wong, Joseph Wong, Wayland Wong, and Peter Yuen) formed the Fellowship of American Chinese Evangelicals (FACE). FACE sought to stem the tide of church and ministry dropouts among the American-born Chinese Christians, and strategized to provide solutions for ABCs and the Chinese churches. NACOCE became a vehicle for further ministry. The Chinese church structure took shape on this continent.

With the "institutionalization" of the Chinese church in North America, a new face emerged. Chinese Christians became more prosperous, more successful in their ministry, and more equipped for outreach. Despite all of this, there seemed to be little effort to relate the gospel to the Chinese church's surroundings, North American society in general, and the Chinese community in particular. The time-honored model of "rejection and denial of culture" persisted, and those who sought to go beyond this mostly reached a stage of "juxtaposition of Christianity with secular culture." This began to change in the 1990s as American ministries such as Promise Keepers and Focus on the Family began to impact Chinese Christians in North America. With all this, we still await a true breakthrough with the power of the gospel in the realm of culture. Meanwhile, American-born Chinese largely lay outside the ministry of the Chinese church.

The Computer Age (1980 — present)

In 1979 President Jimmy Carter established diplomatic relations with the People's Republic of China. The geopolitics of the world revolved around what happens in Beijing as well as in Washington and Moscow. The influence of Islam and Arabic oil-producing countries became increasingly evident. Following the civil rights movement in America, particular lobbying groups became increasingly audible: women, gay and lesbians, ethnic minorities, senior citizens, and the disabled, just to name a few. America no longer perceived herself as a melting pot, assimilating every newcomer group; rather, she saw herself as a world of communities. Ethnicity became accepted, popularized, and even powerful. Finally, in industry, education, medicine, and *almost every area of life*, the computer became omnipresent. *Time* magazine substituted its "Man of the Year" with "Machine of the Year" in 1982: the computer. Sociologists and futurologists proclaimed the end of the industrial age and the beginning of the "information age."

Chinese immigrants continued to flow into the large cities of North America. Canadian cities such as Vancouver and Toronto, and U.S. cities such as Houston, made the overall picture of Chinese communities more diverse; the presence of immigrants and students from the People's Republic of China, Singapore, and Malaysia, made the profile of the Chinese community more complex. Professionals who formerly lived in the suburbs were now moving into the city as part of the "Renaissance" or urban renewal plan. Restaurant workers moved from Chinatown to more outlying areas, sometimes commuting to work in a small town, living there for six days of the week, and returning home to see their wives and children once a week. The city/suburb distinction became more blurred. The diversity and multiplicity of dialects and subcultures became more even in distribution. Chinese were by no means assimilated into American society, but they were more evenly distributed across the North American landscape.

While many Chinese continued to feel the pains of being a minority person, some were moving into positions of power and influence. Increasingly Chinese women were entering the professional schools — law, medicine and business. Middle-echelon management positions were no longer difficult to attain. In the 1980s and 1990s, being Chinese (or being "Asian") was becoming acceptable; Asians became the envy of other minorities in America.

The 1980s was a very private, pragmatic age. There was no major breakthrough in the realm of ideas. The Chinese evangelical church of North America, likewise, continued previous patterns of ministry, outreach and structure. The crucial question for the Chinese church in North America in the 1980s was leadership. Who will emerge to minister the Word of God? Who will go and proclaim the gospel of grace? Who will stand up and demonstrate justice in society? Who, in other words, will rise into position of leadership?

In the spring of 1982, three separate reports indicated that American education was a total failure. It seemed that the caliber of Chinese students and young people had gone down over the past decade. We were less prone to use our minds; we were more prone to spend time with machines. We were less ready to ask questions; we were more likely to passively receive ready-made answers. Leadership among Chinese Christian youth seemed to remain in the hands of those who were college-aged ten years ago, that is, those in their thirties now. This is a real concern which must be addressed by the Chinese church.

Who will lead the Chinese church? Among the American-born Chinese Christians, many seminary graduates are unemployed, unable to fulfill the Chinese churches' requirement that they speak Chinese. Some churches began to accept the idea of calling an English-only person for their ministry; however, many ABC pastors drop out of the Chinese church. There is an urgent need for American-born Chinese and Asia-oriented Chinese to understand each other in the areas of thought, lifestyle, behavior, motivation, and attitudes in the ministry.

In the 1980s, several evangelical seminaries began to offer courses, majors and degree programs within their traditional curriculum structure to meet the need of culturally sensitive Chinese pastors in North America. Some seminaries were aiming at Asia-born Chinese and their concerns; still others made a serious attempt to study Chinese culture. While these were encouraging signs, and many observers hoped for more coordination and cooperation among these "Chinese studies programs," most of them fell into decline by the 1990s. American and Canadian seminaries, facing economic challenges of their own, failed to demonstrate their commitment to Chinese studies, often relegating them as optional programs. As the twenty-first century dawns and Asia becomes the most strategic region in the world, it is sad that the American evangelical church is ill-equipped to train Chinese, American-born Chinese, and non-Chinese workers to minister in the global Chinese world.

Throughout the 1980s and 1990s, there were hundreds of men and women who made a decision to enter the full time ministry at regional winter/summer conferences. Where are they today, years after such decisions were made? How many Chinese students are there in seminaries and Bible colleges in North America? Chinese seminary students and graduates reflect a small fraction of those who made decisions to go into the ministry. Who will support them, guide them through the training needed, provide them with internship experiences, and call them? There are a handful of groups (two that I know of) which conscientiously seek to support these seminary students. The need is for *every* Chinese church to support them, and to see them through their studies and internship period into their ministry career.

Tomorrow's leaders must be culturally sensitive, biblically sound, and ready and able to relate to a variety of people: Chinese and non-Chinese, young and old, Asia-oriented or North America-oriented. The Chinese church also must face the reality of a multiple staff for the local congregation. Underlying the leadership problem is the issue of what message we are proclaiming to the Chinese people. Will we present a holistic gospel — Christ for the total person, Christ the Lord of the total person? Or will some of the previous schizophrenia continue?

The Chinese church is on the runway, about to take off. The Chinese church is about to enter the front stage of Christendom. Whether she will make it or not will in large measure depend on the leadership which will emerge.

How will churches grow? By involving every Christian in personal evangelism. Not everyone is an evangelist, but everyone can be a witness. Not everyone can preach, but everyone can share his or her faith in Christ. Everyone can be a friend, reaching out with love to his or her neighbor. Churches also grow when every believer is exercising his or her spiritual gift, and there is genuine fellowship and community life in the church. Churches grow when the world can see that Christians not only trust God, but trust each other enough to have constant open communications with one another. The world needs to see homes filled with love and neighborhoods transformed because some Christian has been there.

What will the Chinese church offer to the world in the twenty-first century?

The Present Hour: The Road to Churchhood

The picture in the 1990s is complex. The Chinese churches and Bible study groups have a third partner: the number of parachurch organizations in the Chinese community have mushroomed since the 1980s. The spirit of entrepreneurship has spread from American evangelicalism to Chinese evangelicalism. Distinct groups are formed to meet distinct needs. Into this picture comes the renewed interest among Anglo-American and other ethnic-American evangelicals in reaching the city for Christ. Younger American Christians are ready to take risks and face personal costs to cross a cultural barrier, whether by going abroad (teaching English in China) or staying at home (reaching People's Republic of China students on North American campuses).

It seems to me that at this present hour, the Chinese church faces two sets of challenges. The first set of issues relates to church renewal. Church-parachurch relationships are part of this concern. The second set of issues relate to the maturing of the church to attain adulthood, or what I call churchhood.

Jesus Christ came to build his church. Jesus Christ may return at any moment, but if the Lord tarries one day, the church must behave as if she has a great deal of work to do, for a very long time. Churchhood, or a mature self-consciousness on the part of the church, involves long- term planning. It means that the church is conscious that she exists as a social institution at a given moment in history. She is willing to take stock of her past — including historical studies and archive keeping. She is willing to invest in the future — including theological training, continuous education of the laity and the clergy, and the anticipation of new, unprecedented needs in the future. And she is willing to invest in her young people.

Part of this maturing process will involve the exploration of church polity and administrative models. As dialogue increases across denominational lines, this exploration will become relevant to a variety of churches. The concern of contextualization in mission circles is best understood in terms of this need to maturity into full churchhood. The aim of contextualization is not so much to take what is missing in Western theology and add Chinese cultural adaptations; that may be a means. The end of contextualization must be a movement of God's people in church, proclaiming and applying the Word in its cultural context, ready to anticipate new needs for application, but ready to stand by the historic gospel of Jesus Christ.

For the Chinese church in North America, this maturing involves discipling of Generation X young adults.

Sizing Up The Present

Now that the past has been summed up and the stage has been set, we can move on to size up the present. As a result of the eclectic inheritance of culture, values and worldviews, there are unique challenges and problems in the Chinese church in North America due to misunderstandings stemming from the diversity within the race. One challenge is finding our identity. Chapter Eight will examine the question, "Who are the Ethnic Chinese (EC)?" It shows the many factors that go into defining "Chinese-ness," and the broad spectrum that Chinese-Americans are thrown across as a result of the many strains of tradition described in the last section "Summing Up the Past" Since there is this dynamic spectrum of cultural identity, there will be difficulties in knowing what is "The 'Chinese' Way of Doing Things" (Chapter Nine). All the information to this point has been a prelude to the specific problems which arise in this chapter. Theoretical propositions in the previous chapters are tied to everyday examples. As a result of these conflicts, the Chinese church in North America is actually bi-cultural, or even multicultural, although we are all Chinese. Hence Chapter Ten, "A Bi-cultural Profile of Chinese Church Ministry in North America," looks at this phenomenon.

In this section, you are invited to experience everyday life in the Chinese church in North America.

Who are the Ethnic Chinese (EC)? American-Born Chinese in Global Perspective

My Journey: Coming to Love Ethnic Chinese

Since 1965 I have lived, studied and ministered in North America. I have participated in the struggle and growth of the Chinese church in the United States and Canada as we faced the reality of "American/Canadian-born Chinese," and the challenge of reaching them, discipling them, and raising up leaders from amongst them. I have come to love many ABCs and CBCs. My wife and I planted and served in a church for ABCs from 1980 to 1985. Today, Covenant Presbyterian Church (Whitestone, New York) is a bilingual and bicultural congregation. In 1997, Covenant Presbyterian started a daughter church called Covenant of Grace Church (Elmhurst, New York). And for three years (1992-1995) I served as the senior pastor at the Chinese Christian Union Church of Chicago. One of our nine congregations was the Chinatown English congregation. I learned a great deal from those two hundred twenty American-born Chinese; they loved me and encouraged me as their pastor. It was truly rewarding.

A thorny issue in many Chinese churches in North America has been the cultural differences between overseas-born Chinese (known as "OBCs," those born in Taiwan, Hong Kong, Southeast Asia, and more recently, mainland China), and the American- or

Canadian-born Chinese (known as "ABCs/CBCs"). I have visited many churches where the pastor and leaders feel helpless. "How do we serve ABCs?" they cry out. As we approach the twenty-first century, most Chinese churches have come to accept the reality that English ministries are needed: children, youth and young adults need ministries of worship, education and evangelism in their own language and culture. The key to effectiveness lies in this: OBC pastors and leaders who have successfully reached and assimilated ABCs/CBCs are those who have reached out and partnered with ABC/CBC pastors and leaders. Chinese-speaking OBC leaders must set the example. ABCs are the OBCs partners.

As I participated in CCCOWE conferences in the 1980s, I noticed another trend: there are Chinese-born in Southeast Asia, Europe and elsewhere, whose primary language is not Chinese, and whose cultural orientation is different from OBCs. How do we define them? How do we relate to them? Gail Law coined the term "LBCs" in the early 1980s to refer to the fact that, from the point of view of the host country (for example, Indonesia, Australia or South Africa), they are "local-born Chinese." At the Ethnic Chinese Congress On World Evangelization (Honolulu, 1984), we learned that there are different host countries and cultures. Some, like the United States, have been continuously open to Chinese immigration. Thus, there is a constant influx of OBCs, who in turn give birth to LBCs. In other host countries and cultures immigration stopped (for example, in Thailand, Indonesia and Malaysia). Without a constant influx of OBC immigrants, the LBCs grew up, intermingled (and intermarried) with people of the host culture, and developed churches and ministries in their host language and culture (for example, Thai, Malay/Indonesian, and English in Australia and Great Britain). In some countries, they have done this without reference to OBC church leaders.

We noticed that not all host languages are understandable to Mandarin-speaking leaders: in Tahiti and in Mauritius for example, the Chinese community speaks Hakka and French! It is highly symbolic that many LBCs have non-Chinese names (especially in Thailand and Indonesia). It was a joy for me to meet LBC brothers and sisters at Chiangmai, Thailand in September 1989, as CCCOWE's ethnic Chinese congress ministered to them. A thought began to brew in my mind as I came home from Chiangmai: the very definition of "Chinese-ness" was in need of revision.

During the 1990s China evolved into a global economic power. By 1997, six hundred thousand mainland Chinese (PRC) intellectuals were studying or doing research overseas in North America, Japan, Australia, Europe, and Southeast Asia. Three hundred thousand of them were in the United States alone. The OBC communities now have an added cultural element: newly arrived PRCs. As "overseas Chinese" (both OBCs and LBCs) began to be noticed by Westerners as one of the most strategic and powerful networks (see John Naisbitt in *Megatrends Asia*), scholars began to revise the definition of "Chinese-ness."

In 1987, I thought that anyone who wants to consider themselves as a Chinese is Chinese. In other words, "Chinese-ness" is a form of cultural self-perception. Professor Tu Wei-ming distinguishes between three symbolic universes as he surveys the global Chinese community in *The Living Tree*: first, China, Taiwan and Hong Kong (what is now called Cultural China or Greater China); second, overseas Chinese, or *hai wai hua ren* (better than the older term, *hua qiao*); and third, economists and journalists (and we may add as Christians, missionaries) interested in China. This fits my previous definition of "Chinese-ness" as a self-perception.

As I travel in Southeast Asia in the 1990s, I have come to know many LBC pastors and missionaries. Like ABCs and CBCs in North America, they are not OBCs; but unlike ABCs and CBCs, their host culture is not North American. They are Asians. At the same time, when I take a fresh look at North America's ABCs and CBCs, I find the idea of "Asian-American ministries" taking form. My children's friends in young adult ministry are Koreans, Japanese, as well as Chinese. Students who took my undergraduate classes in Asian history, or who consulted with me about missions, are likewise Asians from various cultural backgrounds. At Wheaton College's 1996 graduation commencement, I noticed that the only two graduates listed under "Hong Kong" as their country of origin, had non-Chinese last names! There is an increasing number of non-Asian young adults growing up in Asia today.

ABCs and CBCs are now part of the larger Asian-American community. New strategies in worship, education and evangelism are being developed. Will OBC leaders understand and accept these new challenges?

As CCCOWE was preparing for its Fifth Chinese Congress on World Evangelization (CCOWE) in July 1996, Rev. Chan Hay-Him, CCCOWE's general secretary, called for a separate track of the congress program for "Ethnic Chinese." "Ethnic Chinese" refers to those whose primary language is not Chinese, and who live in host cultures outside Chinese-speaking areas (that is, outside Cultural China). These Ethnic Chinese are distinguished from Traditional Chinese, at least by the very fact that they need ministry in different languages and cultural orientations. At this juncture I must admit that by Traditional Chinese we usually mean Chinese (Mandarin)-speaking church leaders with ancestral roots in China who have lived much of their lives in Taiwan and Hong Kong (and in some instances, Southeast Asia). This is a definition based only on empirical observation. Incidentally, the overseas Chinese church leaders today (from Taiwan and Hong Kong) were the

PRCs (recent emigrants from mainland China) forty to forty-five years ago! In the coming years, as PRCs become a significant part of the membership and leadership of the Chinese-speaking church, the very definition of "Traditional Chinese" will change again.

One problem for CCCOWE was how to find a common language (and cultural orientation) for all Ethnic Chinese conferees at CCOWE 1996. Will North American-born ABCs and CBCs lead in defining, networking and strategizing for all ethnic Chinese? Where is the Asian factor? Do North American Ethnic Chinese have an adequate common base of experience with Southeast Asian Ethnic Chinese? In any case, for CCCOWE and many mission-minded church leaders, the Chinese church must stand united — Traditional Chinese and Ethnic Chinese, together — for the sake of world evangelization.

The very definition of "Chinese-ness" is in need of revision... again.

Who are They? — Eight Factors in Definition

As I pondered over this often confusing situation, I began to realize that there are eight different factors which contribute to the complex problem of defining "Ethnic Chinese." Although some of these may be obvious to many readers, I trust that this discussion will help clarify the confusion.

Primary Language

From the Ethnic Chinese Congress on World Evangelization (ECCOWE 1984) to the Fifth Congress (1996), we have come to agree that LBCs, or Ethnic Chinese Christians whose primary language is not Chinese, are our brothers and sisters. We have noted above that this non-Chinese language, usually the official language of the host country, can either be European or non-European. We must further distinguish between ethnic Chinese people whose non-Chinese language (for example, English, Indonesian, or Thai) is primary and those who are bilingual (some among them are bicultural). Currently there is a vibrant generation of quadralingual ethnic Chinese pastors and church leaders in the Philippines (they speak Hokkien, Mandarin, Tagalog, and English).

The existence of bilingual and bicultural Ethnic Chinese (LBCs) in Asia (for example, Singapore) and in the West (for example, England), compels us as Traditional Chinese Christians to recognize that we cannot polarize Traditional and Ethnic Chinese into two distinct categories. As Chinese culture is in flux, so is the Chinese church. The existence of bilingual and bicultural Chinese, whether OBC or LBC, has given us a tremendous opportunity to promote partnership and understanding, and to model the unity of the Body of Christ as we cross cultural barriers to bring the gospel to the world.

Immigration History of the Family

Most Ethnic Chinese are second generation or third generation Chinese. "Second generation" is defined by the fact that the "first generation" immigrated to the host country, giving birth to the second generation. In the Korean-American community, the second generation is called "2.0." They have further defined a generation of "1.5" who were born in Korea, and came to North America during their childhood.

In North America there have always been two parallel waves of immigration from China/Asia: a succession of student generations and a parallel history of worker generations. Both students and workers have been coming to the United States since the 1850s. The first Chinese to graduate from an American university was Yung Wing from Yale University in 1854. This was during the Gold Rush when many workers fled difficult conditions in China and came to the United States in search of a better life. Since then, both students and workers have both settled in North America, giving birth to ABCs (Ethnic Chinese).

We must understand that the history of the Chinese church in North America is unique. Another variable is the immigration policy of the host country. In some countries, Chinese immigration has been continuous. In others, there is a period of interruption, (for example, the Exclusionary Act of 1882 [see Chapter Seven]). Then there are countries where immigration stopped (for example, Malaysia, Thailand, and Indonesia). There are other countries where immigration stopped, and now has begun to open (for example, Singapore, where there are one hundred thousand recent immigrants from mainland China today).

With each immigration wave, and with each "closing" of a country to Chinese immigrants, we witness a distinct generation of Ethnic Chinese born to Traditional Chinese immigrants.

Cultural Orientation

Ethnic Chinese usually identify with the culture of their host society, which may be Asian/Two-Thirds World (from Sabah to Brazil), or Western (from Canada to Holland and Australia). As Asia is modernizing at a dazzling pace, the distinction between Asian/Two-Thirds World culture and Western culture is beginning to fade.

Most Ethnic Chinese are citizens of the country of their birth. A small number, however, in certain periods of history, have returned to mainland China and resumed Chinese citizenship (for

115

example, Indonesian Chinese in the 1950s and 1960s). We also notice that the names of many Ethnic Chinese, especially in Thailand and Indonesia, are no longer in the Chinese language.

We have been using the term "bicultural" to refer to those who not only can speak two languages (for example, Chinese and English), but who can move between two cultures (for example, Chinese and Malaysian) with great ease. In recent years I have come to appreciate a new concept called the "Third Culture Persons." Dr. Mary Lou Codman-Wilson of Wheaton, Illinois, is developing this concept into a ministry. Many bicultural Ethnic Chinese are not just bicultural — they have created a third culture which is neither Chinese culture, nor the culture of the host country. This is especially true if Ethnic Chinese are born of one Chinese and one non- Chinese parent (though a biracial marriage is not a necessary factor in producing bicultural children).

If we accept the concept of "Third Culture Persons," we must further refine our strategies to reach, disciple, and raise up leaders from these various Ethnic Chinese people groups.

Some Ethnic Chinese have experienced three cultures (for example, a Chinese born in Taiwan, who grew up in Peru, and then moved to North America for high school or university studies). These are "Fourth Culture Persons." Is the (traditional) Chinese church ready to understand them, accept them, assimilate them, and share with them the love of Christ and the unity of his Body? What a tremendous potential missionary force waiting to be prepared and sent!

Ethnic Chinese Lifestyles: Modern, Post-Modern

When Ethnic Chinese clash with their traditional Chinese parents, very often it is a clash between traditional Chinese culture and modern (or Western) culture. The Broadway musical,

"Fiddler on the Roof," is a helpful illustration. The poor Jewish farmer in Russia has to agonize over his daughters' wedding plans: one asks for the father's permission and blessing in marrying a poor Jewish tailor; the second asks for the father's blessing only (not permission!); the youngest elopes with her groom. From traditional to modern, we see a continuum (a spectrum) of possible lifestyles. The overseas Chinese church is like this farmer: the difference is, it is as if all our daughters want to get married on the same day! We have every shade of lifestyle, from traditional to post-modern.

What does "modern" mean? The Lausanne Committee on World Evangelization has conducted a study on "modernity." One of the most important characteristics of being "modern" is free choice: we can choose, for example, what to eat, how much to eat, where to eat, how frequently to eat, and whether to eat (or lose weight!). Choices characterize the life of a modern person.

When we say that Ethnic Chinese people are "modern," we must qualify this further. Some Ethnic Chinese are modern with a tendency to identify with traditional Chinese culture (for example, those American-born Chinese who can speak Chinese with a great measure of ease, or who spent a significant number of years in Asia during their childhood). Other Ethnic Chinese are modern, with a tendency to move toward post-modern culture. As a matter of fact, many Ethnic Chinese are already thoroughly post-modern. Interestingly, post-modern Ethnic Chinese can be found not only in New York, but in Hong Kong and Beijing!

As Chinese churches struggle with worship (music) styles, we witness the clash between traditional, modern and post-modern cultures. As more Ethnic Chinese become comfortable with traditional Chinese culture (not because they reject modern culture, but because they choose to appropriate Chinese culture

117

into their lives), there is hope that traditional, modern, and post-modern may be bridged.

Meanwhile, we need a massive educational campaign to help many traditional Chinese pastors and parents understand the contemporary post-modern phenomenon. "Generation X" are children of divorce — many of them are grandchildren of divorce. They grow up in a broken world and a broken home. We — the adult generation — are turning over to them a country with a skyrocketing national debt, crime in the cities, drugs and condoms in the schools, and an uncertain economy. The spiritual condition of the United States (and of the West in general) is horrible. Generation X people know this. And they are especially hungry for relationships. Urbana 1993 and Urbana 1996 were geared for this generation. In some places (like Wheaton College, spring 1995), their relationship with God broke forth into a spiritual awakening!

Will the Chinese church — the entire Chinese church — reach out to them, on their terms?

Attitudes Toward Traditional Chinese Culture

In the 1970s and 1980s, American-born Chinese sociologists Stanley and Gerald Sue helped us understand ABCs more clearly by delineating three possible attitudes ABCs may hold toward traditional Chinese culture.

The first type of ABCs have a "traditional" orientation. They are comfortable with Chinese language and culture; or perhaps they are conditioned to become comfortable by family and school. (For example, some ABCs have spent a number of years in China.)

The second type of ABCs have a "reactionary" attitude toward Chinese culture. They go to a Chinese language school and hate the experience. They reject Chinese culture. In the 1960s and 1970s, many ABCs held this attitude.

The third type of ABCs have fully assimilated into American culture. For them, Chinese culture is not an issue; it is not part of their conscious adult life. Many ABCs of this type marry non-Chinese. They do not visit Chinatown. They have no need for the Chinese community.

When I moved from New York in 1992 (where there is a large Chinese community of over three hundred thousand) to Chicago (with sixty thousand Chinese), I noticed more ABCs of the third type. However, as America turned generally conservative in the 1990s, I have noticed that the first type of attitude is dominant. As I spoke to InterVarsity student groups at Yale, Brown, Northwestern, University of Chicago, and University of Illinois, I found American-born Chinese college students welcoming me and identifying me as an OBC church leader. They were are not ashamed to tell me their OBC church background. Many of them were studying Chinese at the university. One group organized a course on their own, studying the history of missions in China. Some went on to work in Asia/China in kingdom ministry.

It is naturally encouraging for me, a bicultural OBC North American Chinese, to see that ABC college students are not rejecting Chinese culture, but are willing to work with Chinese culture and with the Chinese church. However, this is a gift from the Lord, not something we can coerce by social engineering. (If we try to engineer it, we may reap tragic consequences, as the interview with Jacob Lau in Chapter Two shows.)

Some traditional Chinese parents and pastors force their children to adopt and identify with Chinese culture. This is true especially of recent immigrants from mainland China and Taiwan.

119

The young people, however, will grow up by the grace of the Lord, to adopt any one of the three attitudes. They may adopt their parents' preferred option, or they may not. As Ethnic Chinese move into adulthood, parents will lose their control or influence over which option their children will adopt. Parents can only pray that the Lord will turn the hearts of their children toward home — but cultural orientation is ultimately not something they can choose for their children.

Marriage Partners

How would I react if one day my children brought home a non-Chinese fiancé/fiancée? It may or may not happen, but whether I prefer this or not, I must be ready. For many Chinese parents, they cannot entertain such a possibility.

Many Ethnic Chinese will marry a Chinese partner. It is interesting that, in many churches where Traditional Chinese and Ethnic Chinese work well together, we find that they intermarry. In the church which my wife and I planted in New York City, the present pastor and several other ABC men married Chinese-speaking women. The ABC men have adapted to the traditional Chinese church and community (the pastor drives his wife to practice Cantonese opera!). The Chinese wives, on the other hand, have adapted to their husband's Americanized lifestyle. Both Cantonese and English are spoken in the home, interchangeably (more Cantonese by the wives, more English by the husbands). In Singapore and the Philippines, I have also noticed Traditional Chinese and Ethnic Chinese intermarrying. To me, this is a healthy trend; it bridges the two subcultures for the church and the community.

A great number of Ethnic Chinese, of course, will marry other Ethnic Chinese from their own host culture (for example, American-born Chinese with American-born Chinese). As this continues to happen, churches need to be ready to reach, disciple and raise up leaders within each specific Ethnic Chinese community. Ethnic Chinese churches will continue to be needed. This has been the need in the United States and Canada. This need has been successfully met in Singapore and Indonesia (where the Ethnic Chinese churches are larger, and greater in number, than the Traditional Chinese churches!).

Many Ethnic Chinese will marry a partner who is a Westerner, or a non-Chinese Asian, or a spouse of mixed racial origins. My prayer is that, as interracial marriages become more common around the world, the entire Chinese church will learn to accept, embrace, love, and share with these dear brothers and sisters. Let us shed our Chinese prejudices and truly practice the unity of the Body of Christ.

Where Do Ethnic Chinese Worship?

As I travel beyond the confines of OBC churches in North America, I am amazed to find Ethnic Chinese in a variety of churches and worship services:

A number of Ethnic Chinese worship in a Chinese-speaking worship service. They do so either because there are no Chinese churches with worship services in their primary language, or because they make a conscious choice to identify with the Chinese-speaking church. Still others are there (especially children and youth) because their parents want them to worship in Chinese.

Many Ethnic Chinese worship in a bilingual service. The entire service is translated between Chinese and the host country's language (English, Indonesian, and so forth). Translation is necessary, in some places, because of government regulations; in others, it is done because there is a shortage of pastors for the Ethnic Chinese.

Many Chinese-speaking pastors and church leaders prefer translation in order to keep the entire church family together. They prefer this to separate worship services in English. (Whether or not to have a separate English congregation has been a controversy among Chinese churches in North America since the mid-1970s; today most churches accept the fact that an English worship service is necessary.) These bilingual services are mostly influenced by Traditional Chinese culture and spiritual styles. The music is oriented toward the traditional style — the gospel songs of the nineteenth and early twentieth centuries. The platform leadership — worship leader, song leader, choir members, and the person making announcements — is dominated by Chinese-speaking adults. I worshiped in such services in Toronto, Canada, and suburban Chicago, Illinois.

Then there is another type of bilingual service which is oriented toward the host country's culture (or modern culture). In one Chinese church in Singapore I worshiped in a service which, for all practical purposes, followed modern styles and forms. The music was a combination of traditional hymns and contemporary music drawn from the 1970s and 1980s. In this particular congregation, Traditional Chinese and Ethnic Chinese worship together, and many intermarry. A few non-Chinese can be found in the worship service, too. I predict that worship services such as this one will move toward the non-Chinese cultural pattern in the next ten years.

The point is, while some Chinese churches prefer bilingual services in order to preserve some measure of Chinese culture, these bilingual services may, over the course of time, develop into non-Chinese-speaking forms.

In North America, English worship services have been a trend in the past ten to fifteen years. If we take a longer historical perspective, we will understand that many Chinese churches have had English-speaking young people since the first half of the twentieth century, and services tended to be bilingual. Then came the immigration wave of the 1960s and 1970s, and the needs of the English-speaking young people became relatively neglected, until a chorus of concern began to be heard all across the United States and Canada. Now, separate English worship services, featuring contemporary music by worship teams, can be found in many cities. Compare this with the contemporary phenomenon in Singapore and Indonesia: the English worship services have developed far beyond the Traditional Chinese cultural patterns. In many instances, these English speaking mega-churches are making a significant impact in their country and around the world. In North America, American-born Chinese are planting churches to reach their neighbors, regardless of cultural background (for example, in Los Angeles).

Can we still call these churches "Chinese churches?" What does it matter? Christ is proclaimed, and for this we need to rejoice, and again rejoice! It is noteworthy that pastors such as Rev. Lawrence Kong of Singapore, have taken intentional steps to reach out to the Chinese-speaking churches with words of repentance and reconciliation — what a role model! As Chinese-speaking church leaders, we need to reach out to them, and thank God for how he has used our brothers and sisters beyond our Chinese-speaking church walls. When will Traditional Chinese leaders reciprocate Rev. Kong's gestures of peacemaking?

In many places in the world, we can find Ethnic Chinese in Western, English-speaking churches. In North America, of course, this means the mainstream-culture American/Canadian churches, often with a Caucasian majority. In other places — from Hong Kong to Beijing to Washington, D.C. — we find "international churches" seeking to reach people from around the world.

We thank God that these congregations are reaching out to "internationals" or "expatriates." In these congregations we will find Ethnic Chinese and, very often, Traditional Chinese. This is mission! This is mission work "from Jerusalem!"

How Effectively Have the Ethnic Chinese Been Reached?

In certain parts of the world Ethnic Chinese are well evangelized. Witness the fact that in some medical schools in Singapore the vast majority of the students are Christians. In other parts of the world, however, evangelizing the Ethnic Chinese has been a struggle — an outstanding example would be in the United States. In still other parts of the world, evangelizing the Ethnic Chinese is a new pioneering work — for example, in Great Britain and South America.

The Dynamic Bicultural Continuum Model

These eight factors can be thought of as spectrums, with a given Chinese-American or Chinese-Canadian at any point on each spectrum. However, pinpointing cultural orientation is even more complicated since we are constantly moving along this spectrum throughout our lives.

At ECCOWE 1984, it was brought out that the place of birth of a person is not the determining factor of a person's attitudes, perceptions and behavior. Rather, it is the cultural orientation of that individual. Dr. Gail Law has developed this thought in terms of a "Dynamic Bi-cultural Continuum Model," presented by her in *NACOCE Bi-monthly* (September 1984), and *Theology News and Notes* (Fuller Theological Seminary, October 1984). The idea is that every person is "on the move" somewhere along a continuum, ranging from Chinese-ness on one end, to American-ness or indigenous cultural orientation on the other. The concept of a continuum is most helpful. It opens up possibilities for studying the seemingly infinite variety of Chinese people. However, it takes much effort for church leaders to accept this concept and to begin thinking in this way accordingly. It is not comfortable because it allows for little or no stereotyping. Reality becomes a matrix, not a dualism.

One summer I had the opportunity to visit with an ABC friend who is pastoring a congregation of fourth- and fifth-generation ABCs. He was astonished to discover how "China-fied" his church members are: how these ABC adults associated mainly with other Chinese in the community, how traditions (such as wedding rituals and beliefs) persisted through to the fifth generation. This "residue" or resiliency of Chinese culture among LBCs was further illustrated at ECCOWE in Honolulu, when Rev. David Chan of Houston shared how he, a third generation LBC, had returned to his Chinese roots. Chinese culture dies hard! Many LBCs, therefore, are more "Chinese" than they realize, or are willing to admit. At the same time, most OBCs, one must say, are more "American" or "indigenous" than they are prepared to face up to. Clarence Cheuk's experience during his summer trip to Hong Kong is a good illustration (Chapter One). We are all "on the move" in the bi-cultural continuum.

In the 1980s, our congregation in New York struggled with the question whether cultural differences were real, or only perceived. For example, some ABCs (more than others) were on very friendly terms with OBCs. There seemed to be no problem sharing and fellowshipping. There were other ABCs and OBCs, however, who would be more comfortable if put in a mono-lingual setting for fellowship. Why is this the case? Is it perhaps because everyone is somewhere in a continuum, and those in the middle of the continuum (whether slightly to the side of "Chinese- ness" or to the side of "indigenous culture") find it easier to communicate with others in the same "middle zone?"

We can push the issue further and ask whether differences in the church are really due to culture at all. Any two fallen sinners (we all are sinners and are only saved by the grace of God in Jesus Christ) would become "incompatible" with other sinners. There is no perfect compatibility, whether between spouses or between Christians in a church or fellowship situation. There are definite personality differences between individuals. What does this mean? Does this mean that on top of cultural differences we have personality differences (cf. Genesis 3:15; 11:1-9)? Or are the purported "cultural differences" really personality differences?

These problems bring me to ask again, what is "Chinese-ness?" There seems to be no contemporary model of pure, static Chinese culture. Everyone is affected by westernization, modernization, urbanization, immigration, and the mass media. So who is a "Chinese?" What makes a person "Chinese?" When Chinese Christians in Australia, South Africa, and Indonesia work together on multicultural teams with brothers and sisters from India and other parts of the world, when do we stop talking in terms of a "Chinese ministry," or "Chinese Church?" What if the LBCs do not identify themselves as "Chinese," but rather, for example, as Singaporeans and Australians? Are the OBCs willing to accept this "new reality" which is beginning to haunt us (although it has been on the horizon for years, perhaps decades, in certain countries)?

Diversity and change are disturbing realities. Perhaps we need to admit our inadequacies, and see whether the Bible also offers a dynamic (rather than static) model of cultural progress. Is God "dynamic" or "static?" Are we willing to entertain the possibility that cultural diversity and cultural change are realities which the Bible faces, accepts, and deals with — albeit in God's own way? Perhaps we all need to do more homework and study the original cultural contexts of the Bible — both the Old and New Testaments. Biblical studies should be part and parcel of the study of indigenous theology and indigenous ministry.

Culture: Is it the Issue?

In the aforementioned situation of our church we were asking the question, "Why do people find it difficult to communicate with, and get along with each other?" Is it because of culture? More pointedly, is it only because of cultural differences? What about personality? More basically, what about sin? In what sense is the basic problem spiritual, with the answer lying in one's relationship with Jesus Christ and the spiritual ministry of every believer?

There are many personality theories; for example, take the four personality types model. One can speak of people as dominant (extrovert, task-oriented), influential (extrovert, person-oriented), steady (introvert, person-oriented), or competent (introvert, task-oriented). In terms of "synchrony" between organizational structure and individual work performance, one could classify people at work as producers, processors, or integrators. The question is, do we find all personality types or individual work styles in every culture? If so, do we need to draw graphs correlating personality and culture (see Fig. 1)?

When one begins to examine the cultural differences between people groups (for example, pragmatic vs. conceptual, relational vs. task-oriented, mystical vs. cognitive, introvert vs. extrovert), are we not dealing with personality differences? The question needs to be asked, in what sense do cultures differ from one another (thus the importance of anthropology is readily seen), and

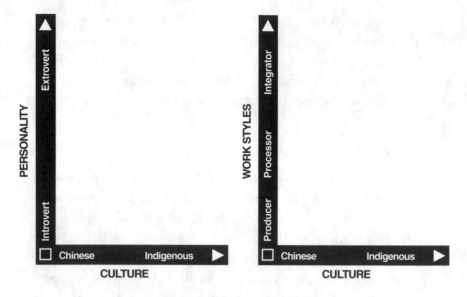

Figure 1

in what sense are they similar to each other (thus the importance of integrating theology with anthropology is apparent)? Missiologists Samuel Rowen and Harvie Conn have been raising this issue in the past twenty years. Can we draw the continuum as overlapping (See Fig. 2)?

Having asked the question, "In what sense are cultures similar?" we need to return to the issue of intercultural differences. There *are* distinctives. An English-speaking fourth-generation ABC is different form a Chinese-educated, Mandarin-speaking immigrant who has just arrived from Taiwan or from mainland China. Perhaps we can at least say this much: although the place of birth is not the primary determining factor for a person's attitudes, perceptions, and behavior, the language (or languages) a person speaks (in which a person thinks) is often a fair indicator of a person's cultural orientation.

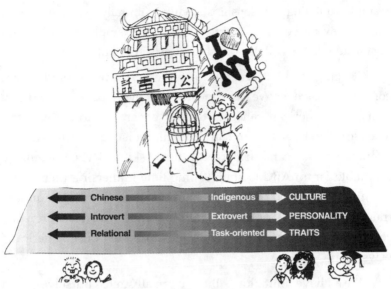

Figure 2

Language is not the only determining factor for cultural orientation, but it plays an important role. Language carries thought forms, symbols, and beliefs; different languages involve different thought processes. Thus we can speak of "culturally more Chinese" or "culturally more American" persons when we note the fluency and ease with which language, be it Chinese, English, Spanish, or Indonesian. The situation becomes complicated when more than one language is used: Hakka and French (as in Tahiti); or Taiwanese, Portuguese, and English (as by the people who were born in Taiwan, grew up in Brazil, and are now attending college in the United States); or different styles of English (as by an Australian-born Chinese living in South Africa).

If language/culture and personality/work types fall on the same overlapping continuum, we can begin to say that culturally more Chinese people may be stronger in certain aspects of the ministry, (for example, building relationships), while culturally more American people may be better at other aspects (for example, planning and organization). We will draw such contrasts in Chapter Nine.

If language/culture and personality/work styles are correlated, however, we can conclude that every person, culturally Chinese or American, can learn to be a "generalist" in the ministry: a task-oriented person can learn to build personal relationships; a relational person can learn organizational skills. Thus, it would be profitable for an ABC to spend some time immersing themselves in Chinese language and culture, perhaps as part of their seminary training; or an OBC or a PRC interning in an American Christian community, thus exposing themselves to more "pure American" ways of life.

We all have limitations. But we can all stretch ourselves, with God's grace. Can we live with both realities?

Cultural Diversity: Making Law's Dynamic Bi-cultural Model Two-Dimensional

Dr. Gail Law's dynamic bicultural continuum model describes both the variety of possibilities in a person's cultural orientation and the process in which a person is changing. It is important for us to keep in mind that the continuum is both a spectrum and a process. No one stands still. We are all on the move (for source refer to the section "The Dynamic Bicultural Continuum Model" in this chapter).

And yet we have to remind ourselves that ABCs are sometimes more "OBC" than they realize; and, OBCs, are almost always more Americanized than they realize or admit. Why is this so? I would like to suggest that, if we make Law's bicultural continuum two-dimensional, we will begin to see why we are all more American, or more Chinese, than we realize.

The "cultural orientation" category can be broken down into two components: the first, for the lack of a better term, is a person's "socialization." This includes a person's family upbringing, language training, cultural exposure, crisis events, and so forth. This is what makes a person what he or she is, based on his or her past background. A person's cultural orientation, in terms of socialization, definitely finds itself somewhere on Law's bicultural continuum.

The second component is, also for the lack of a better term, a person's "self-perception" or "identification." Does a person see themselves as a pure American? As a half-and-half? A both-and? A pure-blooded Chinese? A person's self-perception can be different from, and independent from, a person's socialization. Crisis events and intervention points in a person's life experience can make a tremendous impact, and thus shift a person's self-perception (in terms of cultural orientation) significantly. For example, a foreign student from Hong Kong, put in the middle of the Deep South or the Midwest in the United States, can become thoroughly American in his or her behavioral patterns and self-perception. An Asian-American (that is, an American-born Chinese) may be thoroughly American in his or her self-perception in high school, but becomes much more aware of the Chinese language, culture and history in college. He or she may join the "Asian-American movement," as in the late 1960s and early 1970s. He or she may take a summer trip to Asia for cultural exposure (whether forced by parents or voluntarily). Thus a person's self-perception may be different from a person's socialization; or rather, a person's socialization may change in such a significant way, that his self-perception will change also.

The point I would like to make is that a person's self-perception, that is, the point on the dynamic bicultural continuum, is not always identical with a person's socialization. What we have is a two-dimensional bicultural continuum model (see Fig. 3). On the x-axis we have socialization and the y-axis, self-perception. If we draw a 45 degree line, we have a continuum of people who are exactly as culturally Chinese, as they think they are. On either side of this diagonal line, however, are the vast majority of Chinese people. There is distortion in self- perception; there is change in self-perception; and we are often more American, or more Chinese, than we realize.

Most of us, however, do not stray too far from "the line of consistency." Our self-perception is not too distorted. We are only a little more Chinese, or a little more American, than we realize. This makes it relatively easy for us to get along with others in this two-dimensional bi-cultural continuum. We can be somewhat compatible with others. I would like to draw an ellipse around the "line of consistency," and what we have is a "field" of people in the Chinese community in North America (see Fig. 4).

There are those who would argue that their self-perception is "Christian." They do not belong to any cultural category *per se*, but are first and foremost citizens of the Kingdom of God (Philippians 3:20). This is a most biblical concept, and we all need to be more aware of where our priorities and commitments lie, and to see if our action and thinking reflect our prior commitment to Christ and his Kingdom (Mathew 6:33). The point is well taken.

However, having granted that our first identity and priority is Christian, we need to balance this with the reality that we are all more or less Chinese or indigenous, in our socialization. Although our self-perception may be "pure Christian" or "pure biblical," we cannot change our past. Thus for such people, I would draw an area (shaded) in our two-dimensional bi-cultural continuum to indicate that, while their first loyalties are to Christ (in self-perception), they are of various socialization patterns.

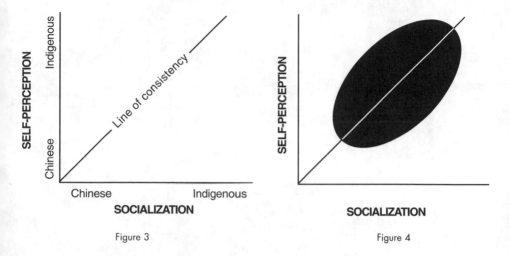

Figure 3   Figure 4

Conclusion

Who is a Chinese these days, and what makes a Chinese truly "Chinese?" This chapter looked at the various difficulties surrounding this question, not only for the Chinese here in North America, but all around the world. Numerous factors can help define the "Chinese-ness" of things, from language, to country of birth, to self-perception, and so forth. But as the reader can conclude, there is as much (if not more) diversity within the Chinese make-up than similarities. The Chinese church must recognize this dynamic when reaching out to the Chinese community here in North America. A Chinese is more than just Chinese culture and values; a Chinese could very well be a blend of many different cultural flavors. Therefore, the Chinese church must have open arms in receiving such diversity if she is to become effective in God's mission to the world.

The "Chinese" Way of Doing Things:
Contours of OBC-ABC Cultural Differences

I am not an ABC, but I am a whole-hearted supporter of ABC ministries. I was born in Hong Kong and came to the United States at the age of fourteen. Maybe because my haircut was too long for many OBC church leaders (although too short for some of my ABC brothers and sisters), many people from Taiwan and Hong Kong thought that I was an ABC. Perhaps because they heard me speak English with some measure of ease, they often asked, "Are you an ABC?" I replied in Chinese, "No, I am from Hong Kong." Then, to the ABCs, it was obvious to them that I was not a fellow ABC. When they saw me mingle with OBCs in a mixed crowd and spoke Chinese, they knew that I was from Asia.

When I was in high school and college, pastors and other well-meaning laypeople would often refer ABC young people to me, saying, "Try to help him," or "She needs someone like you." What they meant was, since they — the elder OBCs — cannot handle ABC young people, I, a younger person, should be able to do it. We, the younger OBCs, should take up the huge task of evangelizing and discipling the "young people in the church!" What a challenge! Are we adequate?

Then I became the youth director of a Chinese church. The young people — high school and college age — called me "Sam," and the mature adults called me "Mr. Ling." The young people expected me to understand their plight — "I do not get anything out of the Chinese service!" (echoed in Chapter Two), while the older people expected me to act on their behalf to preserve Chinese culture — "My son does not behave well; you should straighten him out." The adults wanted the attendance at youth meetings, English worship services, and youth Sunday school classes to be maintained and to increase. The young people wanted to have the freedom to explore different ways to do ministry — not to do things in the "same old boring way."

Then I became the pastor of a small bilingual and bicultural church. There were ABC leaders and there were Hong Kong-born leaders. Although we were a very friendly church, there were times when a person's feelings and thoughts were not adequately communicated to another person. After some thought, I concluded that such misunderstandings were due to: (a) pride and the flesh; (b) personality differences — some people were more outgoing, some more quiet; (c) the interests and benefits of different sub-groups within the church were in conflict with each other; and finally, (d) the difference in culture between OBC and ABC ways of thinking.

Sometimes we do not like to admit that we are products of our own culture. We would like to think that we can, by the power of the Holy Spirit, overcome any misunderstanding if we just pray and talk things over. Yet when we are humble and honest enough to reflect on the whole matter, we would admit that we are indeed products of our own culture — OBC or ABC — and are living examples of that culture. When two cultures come together, they are bound to clash. And the Chinese church, as a bicultural institution, is here to stay. For the next fifty years the Chinese church in North America will be bilingual and bicultural. Therefore, let the OBCs (including the newly arrived PRCs) learn the mentality of the ABCs, and let the ABCs learn the mentality of the OBCs.

We are a transitional generation. We grew up under the leadership of OBC pastors and lay leaders. Whether we are OBC or ABC, we have felt the tensions of the two generations and the two cultures. And sometimes because inter-generational differences are not recognized, young people become frustrated and end up in despair. They feel betrayed by the church. Many a time I wept with young adults who felt "burned" by the Chinese church. They tell me that they just do not receive feeding in the Chinese church. And they cannot wait forever until the Chinese church hires an ABC pastor. I try to understand. I weep with them, but what is the solution? Yes, many Chinese churches ought to call ABC pastors, but until they do, how do we minister to these burned and wounded souls? These fallen soldiers need to "lick their wounds," experience healing, and move on to productive ministry for the Kingdom of God. These "burned" and "burnt-out" brothers and sisters need comfort, encouragement and affection demonstrated to them, so that they can love and give once more again. These "warriors for the truth" need to lay down their weapons and experience some peace, so that they can move on to "civilian life" — building up the Body of Christ instead of participating in tearing it apart. All of this "reconstruction" and "rehabilitation" requires some understanding of what I call the "Chinese" way of doing things.

For decades many Americans have looked upon Chinese culture as exotic. On the second day of high school, shortly after I arrived in suburban Chicago in 1965, I learned from my American schoolmate that "Charlie Chan made the best chop suey in town." I did not know who Charlie Chan was, and I did not know what chop suey was. After two days of high school though, I soon found out. Americans have many stereotypes of Chinese people

137

— as inscrutable, as "smart," and so forth. ABCs, likewise, tend to have some stereotypes about Chinese culture. Their exposure to Chinese culture may have taken the form of sitting through Chinese language classes and Chinese sermons in church. ABCs are pressured by their Chinese-speaking parents to study hard, work hard, get good grades, become a doctor, and marry a good Chinese spouse from a good Chinese family.

What is lacking here is a comprehensive view of Chinese culture seen from the point of view of the Chinese throughout the ages. We shall attempt to outline some of the elements of Chinese culture as they find expression in the way people do things in the Chinese church. I write this chapter at the risk of being misunderstood by my ABC and OBC friends. But this is a risk I must take if there are going to be bridges of understanding between OBCs and ABCs. Judging from the response from my readers and audiences in the past ten to fifteen years, this effort is beginning to pay off.

The Bible, Culture and Mission

What is culture? There are many ways to define it. On the surface, culture is the sum of all behavior patterns of a people. For example, Chinese eat rice with bowls and chopsticks, while Americans eat steak and potatoes with knives and forks. Beneath the surface, however, are values: what people think are important to them. For example, many Americans value efficiency and speed when performing a task, while the Chinese value saving face and maintaining personal relationships. Americans value the privacy of the nuclear family, while Chinese value the broad relationships of the extended family or clan.

If we dig a little deeper we find that there are beliefs that people in a given culture share: these have to do with what they think are "right." For example, Americans believe in progress through science and technology. If a firm makes so much profit this year, it must do better the next year. Chinese, however, can often accept much social change — even a political revolution — without either hope or despair. Things come and go; but heaven's (or nature's) ways will not change. The Chinese often take a more resigned attitude toward change.

Finally, at the center of each culture is its worldview: what is "real" to people in that culture. For example, Americans and most Westerners traditionally view humans as the conqueror (or exploiter) of nature. Chinese, however, view humans as the partner, or correlate of nature. A typical Chinese painting portrays tall mountains and deep rivers, with a small fisherman fishing in his little boat, or a tiny lady sewing inside a hut. Humankind is part of nature; his or her destiny is to harmonize with nature. Such is the Chinese traditional worldview.

According to the Bible, culture is humanity's response to its God-given task to take care of the created world and to improve the quality of life (Genesis 1:28 — 2:15). Therefore, human beings created in the image of God (Genesis 1:26-27) and endowed with intelligence and heart set out to create culture. There are good elements in every culture simply because culture is the product of human beings created in the image of God. However, every culture has been tainted by sin since Adam and Eve sinned; culture needs to be judged, cleansed and renewed by the power of the gospel of Jesus Christ (2 Corinthians 5:17; 10:4-5). Problems arise when we confuse the absolute gospel with the relative cultures. The Bible must always be the judge and the criterion for truth in every and any culture. (ABCs use this argument often when critiquing OBC culture; what ABCs need to realize, though, is that American culture is often used as the lens, rather than the Bible, when evaluating OBC culture.)

As Christians and carriers of the good news of Jesus Christ, we take on three roles with respect to culture. First of all, we are servants: we serve those who need evangelization and discipline. Our whole ministry must be "receptor-oriented" rather than only "preacher-oriented." We need to understand the culture of the people among whom we want to minister.

Secondly, we are *bridge-builders*. As products of one culture, we enter upon another to proclaim the gospel, but also to understand the people's culture so that our message may not be distorted or misunderstood. If missionaries can cross oceans, learn the language, and adjust to the food and customs of the Chinese people, just to bring us the gospel, why can't we — OBCs and ABCs — learn to listen to the "language" and to adjust to one another's culture?

Thirdly, we are *ambassadors for Christ*. Our concern is that the message of reconciliation may get across. Our concern is that, while the message is preached, it gets through to the hearer. Real communication must take place, or evangelism is in vain.

There is a price to be paid — the unselfish love of the mind of Christ (Philippians 2:5). Paul would rather be separated from Christ if only he could bring the gospel to his kinsmen, the Jews (Romans 9:1-5). Paul loves the people of his own culture — not out of some altruistic loyalty to Jewish culture, but for the sake of the gospel. (Some Two-Thirds World theologians call this "biblical nationalism.")

But Paul is also willing to look at his own Jewish culture with the searching light of the gospel. He knows that, as a former Pharisee, the righteousness of God is revealed quite apart from and in contradiction to the works-oriented scheme of salvation known as "the law" (Romans 3:21-24). Therefore, Paul's love for the people of his own culture is not uncritical. His love is not blind. It is realistic because it is for the sake of the gospel.

Paul also knows that his commission from the Lord Jesus is to be an apostle to the Gentiles, that he may bring about "the obedience of faith" of the nations (Romans 1:1, 5). Paul has a cross-cultural motive; he has a heart big enough for foreigners.

Finally, Paul looks forward to the day when every culture would come and bow at the feet of Jesus (Ephesians 1:10; Philippians 2:6-11). Thus, Paul claims his citizenship not with Judea or Rome, but with the Kingdom of Heaven (Philippians 3:20). Paul's identity is far greater than his Jewish heritage or his Greco-Roman society. Paul is first and foremost a citizen of the Kingdom of God.

Therefore, as servants, bridge-builders and ambassadors, let us imitate the example of Paul. Let us seek to preach the gospel to the Chinese people — to OBCs and ABCs alike — that souls of men and women may turn to Jesus Christ for salvation. Let us together aim at the discipling of both the OBC and the ABC "nation." And let us aim at the transformation of both OBC and ABC culture by the power of the gospel. Let us work so that an "indigenous" bicultural church — deeply rooted in both OBC and ABC culture — may flourish in North America, embodying the best of both cultures, and obediently and joyfully serving the Lord Jesus Christ.

Our aims, then, are threefold: evangelization, discipleship and culture transformation (see the section "The Goals of Mission" in the Introduction of this book). And it is because we want to see an indigenous, mature, bicultural church raised up in North America, that we seek an understanding of OBC-ABC differences.

The Individual vs. The Group

When the Chinese church tries to evangelize the community it often seeks to reach the individual to the neglect of the family.

For example, a church tries all methods of evangelism: crusades, films, Chinese classes, English classes, Vacation Bible Schools, and the like. And it discovers that the easiest group of people to bring into the church buildings are the children and the youth. So it builds elaborate programs for the youth. Usually, parents of young children are grateful to the church — "My kids need to socialize with Chinese kids," "My daughter needs to learn Chinese," "My son needs to know how to get along with others in Chinese ways," and so forth.

So they bring their children to Sunday school, Chinese class or Vacation Bible School. But when the Chinese church attempts to evangelize a Chinese-American teenager, especially one from a non-Christian family background, conflicts begin to appear. The young person often does not let his or her parents know what is happening — he or she may be shy or unable to express his or her new-found faith in Jesus Christ in the Chinese language, or unable to communicate with his or her parents in an important matter at all! (Jacob Lau's example in Chapter Two may be extreme, but it illustrates the point of communication breakdown.) So what does the church do? It makes demands on the teenage convert to attend Sunday School, worship services, youth meetings, discipleship cell groups, camps, social events, outings... The young person by now develops a whole new set of friends, none of whom his or her parents recognize! No wonder the parents get suspicious of the church. If the new convert's behavior at home improves (helps with household chores, does not talk back or argue with parents), everything is fine. But as the new convert spends less and less time at home due to church activities, the parents feel like they have lost a son or a daughter.

What has happened is that the Chinese church has adopted, perhaps through Western missionaries, a Western cultural concept of the importance of the individual while trying to evangelize a

142

basically Chinese social unit, the family. How much better if the church learns to communicate with the parents from the very beginning of the evangelistic process! How much better if the church, in its evangelistic efforts, seeks to demonstrate to the parents that they are respected and honored as the heads of the home! (Fortunately, we find that this is beginning to happen in some Chinese churches, as *adults* are being reached through prayer and caring ministries.)

Western culture values the autonomous individual; Chinese culture values the cohesiveness of the family or clan. That is why in Chinese culture an individual must not "stand out like a sore thumb." Actions which are perfectly natural in American society — talking about one's achievements and celebrating them, or freely expressing one's feelings in public — would be taboo in Chinese society. Such behaviors may be interpreted as "showing off," "pride," or even worse, "disrespect." (Natalie Leong expressed some of her frustrations with this aspect of Chinese culture in Chapter Two.)

A Chinese-American graduates from college. His or her parents come on campus, bringing Chinese food and talking loudly as they arrive. They complain about the American food on campus and want to know where they can take pictures. The Chinese-American is thoroughly embarrassed and often completely infuriated. "This is my graduation, and you have humiliated me in front of my peers!" What the graduate does not understand is that the family has adopted the graduation event as a communal celebration. The son or daughter going off to college is a communal family affair — the parents have worked hard to pay for the college education with their blood, sweat and tears. Now all that sacrifice is paying off — so it is time for the whole family to celebrate. Two understandings of the same graduation event — one Western, one Chinese — can lead to much conflict.

143

Take a wedding as another example. A Christian young couple is engaged and secures June tenth as the date for the wedding. They have contacted their minister, who agrees graciously to officiate. They have contacted their friends in the youth fellowship, all of whom rejoice with them and volunteer to prepare refreshments, decorate the reception hall, drive the bridal car, take pictures, and so forth. The fellowship even cancelled its weekly meeting on June tenth . All of a sudden, the parents want to change the date because it is "unlucky." Furthermore, they augment the guest list to three times the original size. They insist on an elaborate wedding banquet in the best and largest Chinese restaurant in town. The couple is totally frustrated. They come to complain to the pastor and the youth counselor. What should they do? All the plans are set, and now the parents "pull this one on us."

What is happening, again, is that the parents look upon the wedding as a communal event. They, the parents, are the hosts of the wedding. They decide which relatives and friends to invite because it is they who are bringing into their family a daughter- or son-in-law! To the Chinese parents the bridegroom and the bride seem almost incidental to the wedding; the important thing is that the family is getting married with another family. Therefore, there is bickering over the gifts, whether or not to distribute Chinese pastries to relatives, how many tables of guests are assigned to the bride or groom's family, and how much to tip the waiters. All of these minute details are ways to celebrate the climax of the parents' hard work in raising their children — they are going to get a daughter- or son-in-law, and soon will become grandparents!

The person in American culture needs to empathize with this family-oriented way of thinking. We are a transitional generation. We need to deal with our Chinese-speaking elders in the communal way, and we deal with our peers and our children in the American, individual-oriented way. Such are the pains of living through a cultural transition — and we would experience much joy if we do it as servants of Jesus Christ!

On the OBC side, parents and church leaders would do well to understand the individualism of the more Americanized Chinese. Individual privacy and integrity lie at the very heart of the American cultural value system. It is something the young people grow up with; to deny this is to deny their selfhood. (Thus a college student will never understand why their mother opens their mail or goes into the drawers in their bedroom!)

Theory vs. Relationship

The young people in a church demand an English-speaking service. The pastor and older laypeople think that the better solution in meeting the needs of the "young people" (even though these "youth" are in their thirties and have children of their own!) is to have the Chinese service translated into English. The ABC young adults feel that they will not be properly fed from Scripture if they have to sit through a bilingual service. So they list reasons why there should be an English service. The pastor is handed this list. He responds with bouts of anger. "Don't you know that this is a Chinese church?" he roars. "You are Chinese! You should speak Chinese! And we are doing you a favor by translating the service into English! What more do you want?"

The young adults, feeling humiliated by such an unsympathetic shepherd, gather together to lick their wounds. Some draft proposals to start an English service despite the disapproval of the church authorities. Others leave the church and begin attending an English-speaking church nearby. Still others — unfortunately a lot of them — leave the church, never to attend another one again.

I am not trying to determine the pros and cons of an English service here. What I am trying to describe, however, are two different ways of looking at a situation. Again, the difference lies in the two cultures: Chinese and American.

The American way of doing things says that when you face a problem or when a need arises in a group, you make a study. You look at what the concrete needs are, what are some of the options in solving the problems, and which is the optimal way to meet the need. Then you write up a proposal, listing the costs and benefits, and present the proposal to the board. And if the board is half-way intelligent, it should buy the proposal, with funding coming from the budget. This is the way things are done in any American corporation; this is the way things should be done in the church as well.

The Chinese way of doing the same thing is by recognizing that there is a problem. There are needs to be met. Now, as we try to find a solution to meet these needs, how can we do so without offending anyone? How can we preserve the unity of the group? How can we make sure that the pastor continues to command the respect of the young people? How can we make sure that the two congregations which will emerge — Chinese-speaking and English-speaking — will get along with one another? How can we prevent clique-ishness? Very importantly, whose "face" will be lost? Who will suffer a sense of insecurity in the process? How will the older people fit into the new scheme of things — will they feel out of place? We have always done things in this way — preserving face for everyone, especially that of the pastor and the board. "Naturally" this is the way to handle the situation with the ABCs. The Confucian/Taoist minds of the Chinese define themselves only in relation to others. Through the concept of *ren* (benevolence, humanity), they strive to preserve social harmony in human relationships.

The American looks at the theoretical foundation of the projects they undertake — "Is this the *right* thing to do?" The person immersed in Chinese culture looks at the interpersonal relationships which would be affected by any new project — "Is this the *best* way to do it?"

If the Chinese church, a bicultural institution, is to survive the next fifty years, we must learn to compromise between the two ways of doing things.

Difference vs. Equality

The bilingual Chinese church is having a board meeting. The meeting is held in English. An English-speaking person is discussing the pros and cons of a new proposal. He turns to the pastor and says, "We believe that this proposal best meets the spiritual needs of our English-speaking people." And he fully expects the pastor, who is awkward in English, to respond with his own set of pros and cons on the issue. What the English-speaking person expects is a genuine debate to ensue. He has treated his pastor as an equal because he treats everyone else in society as equals. He talks to his boss at work this way, so naturally the pastor is addressed in a similar fashion.

The pastor feels humiliated. He remains silent for a while, then mumbles something to the effect that "you young people do not really understand the situation." What the pastor is trying to communicate is, "I am the pastor. Do not treat me as your equal; treat me with respect. And if you respect your elders, you do not talk to them like this!"

For thousands of years Chinese people have been accustomed to a hierarchical way of leadership. There is the emperor on top, with different gradations of government officials. On the local level there are the landowners (gentry) who act as the middlemen between the peasants and the local government official. Everybody knows who the "big men" are in town — the heads of the landowning households. And they are addressed as *da ren* (in Cantonese, *dai yan*), meaning "great person." In another sphere of life, students address their teachers as "master" or "teacher" (*xian sheng*, or in Cantonese, *sin sang*). Even after the student graduates, he or she still addressees the former teacher as *xian sheng*. The student's parents continue to address the former teacher as *xian sheng*, always finding ways to show gratitude for having nurtured their son or daughter. Such is the way the Chinese look upon a person who exercises some leadership role in society.

The Americanized Christian looks upon the pastor as a friend. The pastor is an equal in Christ — we are all equal in Christ. The culturally Chinese Christian looks upon the pastor as a leader. The Christian layperson may gain some access into the personal life of the pastor, befriending the pastor and his or her family. But when the group is discussing official business, there is an invisible line drawn — the pastor's opinion is to be respected and never contradicted in public. From the pastor's view, he or she expects the younger generation to show respect and loyalty to him or her. In his or her mind, loyalty to the pastor and faithfulness to the ministry of the church are one and the same thing.

At one Chinese church, an ABC youth pastor was chastised by his fellow OBC pastors for allowing the high school kids to call him by his first name. The older pastors felt the need to teach the young people to respect their elders and to know their place in the social heirarchy. So the ABC pastor publicly requested the English fellowship to call him Pastor Eng.

ABCs need to show sufficient respect to OBC pastors in order to establish rapport and communication. Once the pastor is assured that the ABC is loyal, he or she will grant numerous requests. OBC pastors, on their part, need to accept the more egalitarian way in which American organizations operate. They need to find their security in Christ and not feel threatened just because a young adult fails to show him or her the proper respect (which only a person immersed in traditional Chinese culture would appreciate).

Love vs. Respect

When Americans want to show affection and love toward each other, they may jump up and down, hug, and kiss each other. When a Chinese-American goes to school in America, he or she is exposed to this way of publicly displaying affection. In one Hispanic Bible study I led in the 1980s, a young lady was late for the study; before she sat down, she hugged everyone in the room! However in the Chinese home, the Chinese-American finds that his or her parents rarely show affection toward one another, and almost never to the children. The young person concludes that his or her parents are cold and are too wrapped up with work at the restaurant/factory to care for the children. All the children ever get are admonitions to study hard, get good grades, become a doctor, and so forth. And the children are expected to abide by certain rules, rules such as eating a bite of rice first at the beginning of a meal, or greeting someone as "Uncle so-and-so" or "Aunt so-and-so" when there is a visitor at home.

Such rules and regulations make a Chinese-American weary. When the young person brings a friend home, he or she is further embarrassed by how the mother piles food on top of the visitor's rice bowl and insists, "You must eat! You are a growing young person! Eat!" But the young person is thinking, "Doesn't Mom know that we know how to use chopsticks, and we can get our own food? And doesn't she know that this is too much for anyone to eat, without getting indigestion?"

Rules and regulations are ways the Chinese community preserves harmony, order and respect. Think of "respect" as the Chinese equivalent of "love." If you really love your parents, you study hard and say "Good Morning, Father" every day first thing in the morning. When you enter the living room, whether leaving the house or coming back home, you always address "Father" or "Mother" before moving on with your business. Such respect is appreciated by the elder person; he or she concludes, "This young person is a really good person; he/she will go far. I like him/her."

Westernized Christians express their love and friendship to one another by playing sports together, inviting each other over for barbecue dinners, holding bridal or baby showers for each other, and going camping together. All of this is foreign to traditional Chinese culture (though many OBC immigrants are adapting to some of the American customs). This is true in the more traditional Chinese churches as well.

The ABC would do well to express "love" to his or her parents in ways that they can understand, such as bringing the first paycheck home to the parents, bringing home some food (fruits, pastries or meat) from Chinatown, and observing the parents' birthdays. In church, saying "Pastor so-and-so, Good Morning!" would really help to win that pastor over to the ABC segment of the church. (Now respect needs to be complemented with other character traits; but respect, or lack of it, is often the first impression which the traditional Chinese has of the ABC person.) Respect spells love.

The OBCs on the other hand, have a great deal to learn about showing genuine emotions with their family and friends. Love that is never demonstrated may never be received.

Self-Confidence vs. Humility

Americans are used to talking about their strengths and accomplishments. One may add that American Christians are also used to talking about their weaknesses and failures with their friends and increasingly in public. American churches are used to Christians giving testimonies of how God has used them, and the whole congregation rejoices.

The Chinese, however, are used to hiding their accomplishments and accentuating their weaknesses in public. In applying for a job in America, the Chinese is modest by saying, "I know a little about computers," while he or she may hold a master's or doctoral degree in computer science. The American employer expects the applicant to list his or her accomplishments. The traditional Chinese has been trained to hide them instead.

In dealing with traditional Chinese, one must be careful not to be too "flashy" about one's credentials or accomplishments. While giving thanks to God for the ways he is using us, we must be careful to note for our Chinese friends that "In and of myself, I can do nothing." Our admission of our weaknesses is a way we identify with those we talk to. We are saying, "We are equals; I am not your superior."

ABCs are often annoyed by these statements of politeness. For example, while the ABC would say, "Thanks for that delicious dinner and for a delightful evening," the OBC might say, "I am sorry I caused you so much trouble; you must have prepared for this for days." While an ABC master of ceremonies would say to the guests at a banquet, "I am glad you came," the OBC says, "Thank you for giving up your valuable time."

This does not mean that while dealing with OBC elders we must crucify our self-confidence. On the contrary! Those with real self-confidence would be willing to accommodate to the other person's way of doing things in order to win him or her.

A word about security — the OBCs often say that the ABCs have an identity crisis; they do not know who they are, and therefore they suffer from a lack of self-confidence. The ABCs, as a matter of fact, do not have a monopoly on the identity problem. The Chinese race has suffered from a corporate identity crisis for the past one hundred fifty years. Lack of confidence and security has plagued our people as a whole. The Bible tells us that true security comes from the Lord, who is our shelter and our strength. In Christ we are made free.

The world is hungry for security; it takes secure, free people to help make others secure and free. The Christian has the only true source of security. Let us share it with others!

Meanwhile, it would not hurt at all if OBCs (and ABCs too) learn to verbally affirm and appreciate traits and deeds of another person. We are often so generous with reprimands and criticism (or scarcasm), and so stingy with compliments. If this is what being a Christian means, who would want to become one?

It is encouraging to see that Generation X makes encouragement and appreciation an integral part of their lifestyle and relationships.

Organism vs. Organization

The Bible speaks of the church as a Body. It also regards the church as an organization — the Bible gives qualifications for leaders and provides a structure for church leadership.

ABCs are used to organizational structures (see the section "Theory Vs. Relationship" of this chapter). We are taught to think in terms of structures and goals. We learn about lines of authority and hierarchical charts. We define each position in an organization with title and job description, complete with criteria for evaluation. We then organize teams to accomplish objectives and call meetings either to plan or to evaluate progress. We write memoranda, take and approve minutes, write reports, and keep files. We accept people into the membership of the church with ceremony and certificate; we assign them tasks and give them titles. We send our young men and women off to seminary to earn degrees, then we ordain them and call them "Reverend."

All of this is, in some sense, foreign to the Chinese mind. Whereas the Western mindset is oriented to things logical, cognitive and intellectual, the traditional Chinese mind is oriented to either the mystical/natural, or to the pragmatic/social.

The traditional Chinese worldview looks upon humanity as a correlate of nature (see the section "The Bible, Culture and Mission" of this chapter). The object of life is to become fully in tune with nature. Thus poetry and art is an important part of life, but it is not merely decoration for life; it is an expression of life itself. On the other hand, from Confucius we learn the proper ways for a social leader to behave — a prince would rule his people with virtue. Thus, traditional Confucian philosophy is a combination of mystical thought and social etiquette. Neither of the two components — mystical or pragmatic — is particularly logical or cognitive in nature.

Translated into everyday life, this means that the traditional Chinese mind is basically uncomfortable with organization, red-tape, paper-work, official and formal lines of authority, formal membership in an organization, and business meetings. The Western mind is "left-brain" oriented; it is cognitive. The Chinese mind is "right-brain" oriented; it is aesthetic.

What does an ABC Christian do? How could life go on in the church without clearly defined lines of authority and function, without job descriptions, criteria of evaluation, and business meetings? I think here it is not a matter of choosing between having organizational apparatuses or not having them. Rather it is a matter of making sure that the OBC leadership understands what a group is trying to do, before the OBC receives the memo or report, before the formal meeting takes place, before he or she is made aware of the formal lines of authority. Build the relationship, and organizational matters will follow smoothly. Ignore the rapport with the leaders, and no matter how much organizing you do, things will not be understood. Things will not get done.

It is an art to understand the ambiguities of the Chinese way of doing things. And just like any art, practice makes perfect. Spending time with Chinese people will help one understand this ambiguous style. Remember, this "way of doing things" is practiced by the majority of the human race, by most non-western cultures and societies.

Whether one is at home with a cognitive or an aesthetic, a left-brain or a right-brain culture, we need to be "total brain" people, reaching out in wisdom and in love in the name of Christ.

Leadership: Credentials vs. Service Record

People who grow up in Western societies are used to formalized means of recognizing leadership. We recognize a person with an academic degree or a professional license. In church, we recognize a person with a Master of Divinity and who has been ordained. We put him or her in charge of a congregation, and he or she (in many churches) presides over the official board. Such leadership positions are accepted by all who know how the organization works.

In Chinese circles, however, the axiom "Respect is earned, not conferred," really comes into play. Chinese laypeople recognize the pastor as leader not because they have a degree or are ordained, but rather because they have demonstrated themselves to be a leader through years of consistent faithful service. The Chinese responds to a coordinator of clean-up who participates in the clean-up themselves; to a transportation coordinator who also drives and gives rides themselves; to a coordinator of Christian education who also teaches Sunday School well; to a pastor who serves Christ humbly, both in the pulpit and in the janitor's closet. This does not mean that the Chinese church should make the pastor do everything. This is just to say that humble service is what people recognize as a sign of leadership.

Chinese people recognize a leader who can command respect from the group. This is seen, in the case of the pastor, in dynamic preaching which communicates God's truth to the hearers, and in evident filling of the pastor's life with the power of the Holy Spirit. In a way, this is most biblical: people recognize a leader who evidences spiritual gifts, and who shows themselves to be a servant. Gifts and service: they serve as signs of leadership.

A leader in the Chinese mind is a strong person who holds the group together. And people build relationships of respect and loyalty with the leader.

Once a leader, however, a person needs to show compassion and understanding to the people in the group. For example, some OBC laypeople would have a very hard time trying to voice their opinions, especially complaints, to an ABC pastor (or to an Americanized OBC). The pastor will have to reach out and find out what the people are thinking because the people are not always going to volunteer their opinions. Sometimes the pastor or elder has to use another person who understands the laypeople on a more intimate level, to find out what the people are thinking. Just issuing memoranda to the people, asking them to fill out surveys, making a "Suggestion Box," and so forth, would not

155

suffice. There needs to be the personal reaching out to the people — this is what they expect in the leader.

In the case of an OBC pastor and an ABC congregation, the laypeople need to reach out to the OBC pastor and find out how he or she feels and what his or her thoughts are. In reaching out, up or down, we build our credentials as genuine contributing members of the community.

Spiritual Gifts vs. Secular Credentials

We have said that the Chinese way of recognizing leadership is through gifts and humble, consistent service. This is true enough, and quite biblical. However, equally true is the fact that many Chinese have great *secular* expectations of their leaders in addition to the spiritual qualifications.

Westerners recognize a person by his or her academic training and professional experience. A person who qualifies is given a position of leadership. The Chinese mindset, akin to the description Paul gave of Jews (who "look for a sign," I Corinthians 1:24), looks out for a leader whom they not only respect, but also admire.

Some of the Chinese secular credentials, which the Chinese people expect in their leaders, include: age (the older the better); the ability to speak the Chinese language; family background; advanced degrees from universities (increasingly, the Doctor of Ministry is being offered and accepted as a substitute for an academic doctorate); marriage and children (this communicates maturity and stability); a house (evidence of responsibility); and being on a social par with other middle-class suburban professionals.

The age qualification is something we can do nothing about. We become old as the years go by. However, ABCs and other

Americanized OBCs would do well to try to learn the Chinese language in order to communicate with OBC church people, as well as to command their respect. Missionaries from the West learn Chinese in order to go to China; why can't we learn each other's language in order to communicate in a bicultural church? John Naisbitt concludes in his book, *Megatrends Asia* (Asian edition, 1995) by pleading with American young people: Go East! And learn Mandarin.

The secular expectations of the Chinese people may not be biblical. Nevertheless, the Americanized Chinese church leader would do well to recognize that these expectations exist, and they die hard.

Where one can do nothing about some of these credentials, it is best to rely on the Holy Spirit and demonstrate by one's life that he or she has the ultimate of all credentials — the presence of God in his or her life. Sooner or later, God will bring about the response from those people who are serious about God.

Lubrication and Preservation: Implicit or Explicit

Each community or culture has its own values and develops rituals to affirm these values. For example, playing tennis or golf together is a sign of friendship among many Americans. In American society, such rituals of friendship are clearly defined so that each person's privacy is not invaded. In Chinese culture, a very high premium is placed on the affirmation of communal values. Often, the birth of a baby, a wedding, or a funeral is much more than the occasion itself. It is a means of bringing the clan together to affirm the family's cherished values.

Take the wedding reception as an example. The ABC is bored at a wedding banquet in which the uncle of the bride makes long speeches and goes to length to introduce every single relative who is alive, whether present at the banquet or thousands away. Sometimes the pastor is asked to make this speech; more likely than not, he or she is asked to offer a prayer.

To the Chinese, especially the parents of the bride and of the groom, such speeches and prayers are more than a mere introduction of guests and demonstration of gratitude to God for the food. It is a communal affair. The pastor represents God's blessing upon the bride and the groom, and also God's blessing upon the two families.

The Chinese pastor is often called upon to perform a sundry list of non-pastoral functions: to be present at a birthday or "red-egg" banquet, to settle a household conflict, to give advice whether a family should invest in such and such a business, to offer counsel as to which college or major a young person should chose, and so forth. Often the pastor is asked by the parents to "tell the kid to straighten up," to behave, and to respect his or her parents.

All these expectations are placed upon the pastor — and upon any community leader — because he or she has become a symbol of the values cherished by the community. When a Christian recognizes this fact, and uses his or her position for the sake of the gospel, much good may result. When power is abused and he or she gets involved in people's lives for personal profit (for example, helping people apply for an immigrant visa for a fee, or a "red envelope"), the power of the gospel and its credibility is lost.

What the Americanized person needs to understand is the tremendous importance of these rituals of value affirmation for the Chinese family and community. If the gospel is to make an impact upon the Chinese community, indigenous, creative yet biblical ways of affirming Christian values must be designed for the Chinese people, so that they can celebrate the lordship of Christ in a cultural form which they recognize.

Conflict Management: Confrontation vs. Conciliation

Finally, there is the difference in how to resolve conflict. In Americanized circles verbal, direct confrontation is normal and expected. When a person does something wrong, he or she should know about it in person, orally and directly. In Chinese circles, however, direct confrontation is "face destroying." It often tears apart the fabric with which the community is woven.

A more accepted way of dealing with conflict is through indirect conciliation. For example, a person wants to voice a complaint in the church. He or she speaks to a responsible layperson, and that layperson brings up the subject with the pastor or the official board. In all of this, we need both ABCs and OBCs to be bridge-builders, to be peacemakers for the sake of the unity of the Body.

Instead of directly confronting an OBC person, the ABC can employ the technique of first approaching an English-speaking OBC, who understands both the ABC's point of view and the cultural forms of the OBC involved. By going through this route, the OBC pastor's face is saved, and one has won a brother or a sister. Why not? What is there to lose?

The traditionally trained OBC, on the other hand, needs to learn how to "speak up" and make known his or her opinions in front of a group or in a meeting. Such direct communication is necessary for the proper functioning of the Body of Christ (Philippians 2:1-2).

Conclusion

We are living in a transitional age. The OBC leaders in the Chinese church fully recognize that they, too, are living in a transitional age. The future leadership belongs to the English-speaking ABCs. ABCs very often feel that the OBC pastor does not understand this. From my own conversations with OBC pastors for the last twenty years, I find that most of them do understand it.

The problem is that this transition must take its course through a whole generation. Some of us cannot wait that long. I can understand their feelings. However, we are talking about moving a whole culture, deeply entrenched in a millennia old tradition, to a modern, Western style of organization and leadership. It is no small task. It is going to be painful for those who cherish the tradition; it will be a tremendous responsibility for the new generation to pick up the baton.

The baton belongs to the future leaders. Will they be patient and understanding enough so that when the time comes, they will indeed step on to the front stage of the Chinese church?

A Bi-cultural Profile of Chinese Church Ministry

Introduction: The Complexities of the Issue

As we have seen from the previous chapters, there is no specific definition of "Chinese-ness." The Chinese in North America are scattered across a cultural spectrum that has more than one dimension. And not only that, they are constantly on the move within this spectrum. This diversity within the race is manifested in the ways described in the previous chapter, "The 'Chinese' Way of Doing Things: Contours of OBC-ABC Cultural Differences."

As a result, the eight hundred Chinese churches in North America are bicultural, or shall we say, multicultural. Every church is a multicultural community. Indeed, we may say that every Chinese person in North America is bicultural; he or she has both Chinese and Western characteristics. How do we sort out which parts of us are Chinese and which parts are Western? If we have done any self-reflection, we know that this is not a simple matter. When it comes to the Chinese churches, it simply gets more complex.

Chinese culture itself is not a homogeneous entity. Nor is American culture. Each culture is made up of "high culture" (for example, Confucianism in China; existentialism in the West) and "low culture" or "popular culture" (for example, folk religion and festivals in China; fashion, fast food and rock music in the West). Both Chinese culture and North American culture have a highly rational aspect — from Confucianist philosophy, classical poetry, and Mao's dialectical materialism in China, to science, technology and medicine in North America — and a highly anti-rational aspect. The popular culture and the anti-intellectual aspects from both Chinese and American culture have greatly influenced the Chinese church. We are only beginning to shed our anti-theological past, and to explore the meaning of the Bible, theology, and how to live out the Christian life in academia and in the marketplace.

In this chapter we will survey a few aspects of the ministry of the Chinese church in North America — her preaching, evangelism, nurture, and leadership style — and show how we are both Chinese and Western. We do not seek to give a "balanced view," if by balanced we mean giving Chinese culture and Western culture each a passing grade, and listing an equal number of strengths and weaknesses for each culture. Rather, we shall seek to ask whether these elements are in conformity with Scripture. How would the gospel evaluate and judge them? And if modifications are required, let us not shrink back from repentance and change.

The Chinese Church in North America: A Preliminary Sketch

I am assuming that the Chinese church in North America, which we speak of in this chapter, is highly suburban in mindset, even if the church building happens to be located in Chinatown. That is, the Chinese church today is mostly led by professional people who are highly educated and who are sending their children to well-known universities. These college students, whether children of the professionals or visa students from Asia, provide much of the manpower needs of the church. In fact, today's professionals were yesterday's foreign students who have graduated, settled down in North America, and started (or strengthened) Chinese churches. At least one-quarter, and up to one-half, of the members of most Chinese congregations were converted in North America; but the spirituality and leadership styles of these churches remain heavily influenced by the revivalist, fundamentalist, moralist and Assembly Hall traditions from pre-1949 China.

There seems to be three kinds of pastors in these congregations: (1) traditional Chinese pastors trained in Bible schools in Asia, with at least ten years of experience in the ministry, and whose children are reaching high school or college age, or beyond; (2) North American-born Chinese pastors, who are only recently welcomed into Chinese pulpits because pastors and elders/deacons have children who are in college and career age, and they need shepherding; and, (3) bicultural pastors, mostly from Hong Kong, who are bilingual, in their thirties and forties, and are now increasingly moving into leadership in churches which may be one hundred fifty to two hundred in size, or larger.

What are the Chinese and Western characteristics of the ministry of these churches?

Preaching: Exhortation or Exposition?

Traditionally, Chinese churchgoers are accustomed to an exhortative, anecdotal and allegorical type of preaching. The goal of preaching, according to this "Chinese model," is to exhort the congregation to lead moral lives, to develop character, and to "grow spiritually." Stories are used all throughout the sermon.

The tone is mostly authoritative, but sometimes paternalistic. The sermon grows out of the life experience and ministry experience of the preacher. It is light on expository and doctrinal content, but heavy on heart-felt response to the challenge of living the Christian life in real-life situations. For example, one Chinese pastor delivered a sermon on 1 Timothy 4:12 ("Do not let anyone look down on you because you are young, but set an example for the believers in speech, in life, in love, in faith, and in purity."), and somehow tangentially led to the maxim: young people today should learn to go to the bathroom in the morning, not before dinner. This is an extreme (yet nevertheless true) example, but it illustrates the point.

This "Chinese model" has its historic roots in the Confucian ideal of the scholar-sage, whose "communion" with nature (*tian di*) resulted in a mystical kind of wisdom; and in the popular storyteller, whose social function is to pass on social values through historical and mythical stories told from village to village. The pietistic tradition transmitted through American and European missionaries reinforces the practical and anti-intellectual elements of this model. The strength of this model is its emphasis on character development, practicality, one's relationship with God, and relationship with people.

Increasingly, however, younger pastors, both OBC and ABC, are trained in the "expository model" of preaching. I would be very hesitant to label this a "Western model," because some young scholars in the Chinese church would label anything cognitive or intellectual as "Western," and thus an undesirable "cultural baggage" from Greece and Rome. I am not sure that the Bible forces us to choose between exhortation and exposition. Be that as it may, the "expository model" begins with a study of the text of Scripture — often, a study in Hebrew and Greek. Key words and sentence structure of the passage are clarified before the preacher moves on to develop his or her main theme and purpose for the sermon. Then he or she consults a variety of sources for illustrations: contemporary newspaper and magazines, ministry situations, literature, and popular culture. The result is a sermon which resembles, in form, the contemporary popular magazine article. There is biblical (and sometimes doctrinal) content; and the content is aimed at behavioral change through application and illustrations.

The cultural roots of this kind of preaching in Western culture can readily be seen. The professor and the corporate executive in contemporary Western industrial (or post-industrial) society are role models. The professor goes to the original sources to find reliable information and presents it to his or her students. The corporate executive looks at the contingencies of his or her context and develops a strategy to lead the company to achieve certain results. The strength of this kind of preaching is that it is aimed at helping Christians answer certain questions about the Bible, and to live Christian lives in the contemporary world. The weakness of this model is that the preacher often assumes, implicitly, that character development and holy living is enhanced only by biblical and doctrinal teaching. The kind of personal influence and example which is emphasized in Chinese preaching is relegated to "discipleship."

Do we need to choose? Can we combine the best elements from each model? It seems to me that, if pastors are to preach expository sermons that exhort and challenge Christians to holy living and obedience to Christ, they need a life-long process of training, mentoring, prayer, meditation, and study. The younger pastor needs to spend more time in prayer, reflection and learning from older people (including older pastors). The traditional pastor can benefit from a selective use of resources (increasingly available in Chinese translation): books, magazines, tapes, as well as Bible commentaries. It is my impression, based on cursory reviews of traditional Chinese pastors' collections of books (even those pastors who have been strongly anti-intellectual in their doctrinal stance), that this kind of self-development is indeed taking place.

And as we move into the twenty-first century, we need to be keenly aware that the traditional expository style of preaching may not suit the learning style of the majority of Generation X, who are not "linear" in their thinking. Storytelling, the use of drama, art and audiovisual aids, are all needed to make the message come alive. Is East meeting West?

Evangelism: Crisis-Event or Process

Traditionally, the evangelistic program of the church in China, Taiwan and Hong Kong revolved around the annual evangelistic preaching crusade. A famous preacher is brought in, and through the fervent prayers, enthusiastic singing, and powerful preaching of the gospel, a "crisis-event" is created in which the individual is compelled to choose to repent of his or her sins and to accept Christ as Savior. More often than not, the non-believer is brought to the crusade by a family member, a relative, a schoolmate, a colleague, or a friend. Family networks are the background of the invitation to the crusade. The focus of this "Chinese model" is on the harvest. The message proclaimed meets the eternal, other-worldly needs of the individual; salvation is understood as eternal life, emancipation from hell, and the forgiveness of sins. The model reinforces the communal and tribal unity of the Chinese family and the Chinese church. It is other-worldly, harvest-oriented, and tribally-based.

Increasingly, however, a more Western model is adopted for evangelism. This model emphasizes friendship and dialogue between Christian and non-Christian. Campus ministries and other church growth agencies in North America have developed Bible study guides and other aids to enhance this process of friendship evangelism. The focus is on the process. A deliberate attempt is made to find a point of contact — a hobby, a social function (or a series of social functions), an intellectual debate on an issue, or a philosophical or scientific topic. The message is more centered on individual needs rather than on clan and tribal needs. The need for fulfillment, friendship, direction, hope, encouragement, and acceptance are all met by Jesus Christ in the here and now. The emphasis is on the this-worldly, temporal benefits of salvation. The challenge is to take the time to think through the meaning of discipleship before commitment. Evangelistic preaching is seen as only the culmination of a long process of cultivation, ground-loosening, listening, discussing, and loving.

The Chinese model works well with people in difficult situations. The Western model seems to work well with educated people who are more or less comfortable in their situations. Each has strengths and weaknesses. While we must never forget the centrality of preaching (which is a Biblical imperative), we must also develop the gifts of every lay Christian to reach out to his or her friends and neighbors with the love of Christ. Evangelism is a process; evangelistic preaching is also an indispensable element for it is commanded by Scripture. How do we combine the two models?

Nurture for Children Only or Adult Development

Traditionally, the Chinese church thinks of Christian education and fellowship groups as programs for children and young people. Thus Sunday School classes are taught from kindergarten to high school. All kinds of youth fellowships are developed. In this model (prevalent in both Asia and North America), hundreds of young people are lost after they enter college or after they enter the work field. While the front door of the Chinese church is wide open, the back door is not shut either. We are losing a whole generation at a time! According to the Chinese model, nurture is done at the Wednesday evening prayer meeting, in home worship services (a preaching service held in a home), and through pastoral visitation. The pastor does the bulk of the visitations; often a willing spouse (who may be trained in Bible school) helps the pastor in this ministry. The saints are comforted, the sick prayed for, the backslider exhorted, and non-Christians hear the gospel preached to them.

Increasingly, contemporary churches think of Christian education as a life-long process. Adults are seen as people in development. Each stage in life has its own demands and needs. Thus the most obvious addition to many Chinese churches today is the young married couples' fellowship (*kang li tuan qi*). Sometimes a pastor and his or her spouse engage in premarital and postmarital counseling, resulting in a whole group of newlyweds undergoing a process of discipleship. Nurturing single, working young adults is not as easy. Often the mobility of young college graduates, and the fact that the college student more often than not attends school away from his or her home church, results in a very fluid situation. Perhaps one might even say that the concept of loyalty to the local church is eroding among young professionals today. Nurture is understood to take place through small group Bible study and prayer. This has indeed been the outstanding contribution made by campus ministries such as InterVarsity, Campus Crusade, The Navigators, and along the West Coast, Asian-American Christian Fellowship and key Asian-American churches. It has helped the Chinese church come out of her anti-intellectual, anti-doctrinal, anti-theological stance, and has enabled many young Christians to find excitement and help in systematic Bible study.

The Chinese model is rooted in the traditional Chinese family and clan, which sees adults as the focus, and children as appendages. The pastor (who is expected to do a lot of visitations) is the one holding the moral and traditional values of the clan together. He or she exemplifies the "Do's and Don'ts," and maintains pride and confidence in the values of the community. The Confucian heritage, in contrast with Western individualism, establishes the identity of humankind only in relationship to others so that the actions of one individual affects, in no small way, the lives of everyone else in the social unit. The Western model, on the other hand, finds its roots in the school system and the university, in which the total person is viewed in terms of his or her various needs.

Do we need to choose between cognitive Bible study and the Wednesday night prayer meeting? How do we disciple young newlyweds and single adults at the same time? What about couples in their fifties? Seniors in their sixties? A whole "philosophy of ministry" needs to be developed for each congregation, unique to its own situation and needs; we find that this is increasingly taking place in Chinese churches. Pastors are encountering models such as the Small Group Church as many of them enroll in Doctor of Ministry programs, or attend specialized seminars to enrich themselves.

Pastoral Leadership: Glue for Clan Values or Visionary Executive

This brings us to the final point about pastoral leadership. Traditionally, the Chinese see the pastor as a marginal person in society. The pastor is not respected, not well paid, and is to remain in the background. The nineteenth century missionary gathered the early converts in China who were (often as a result of conversion to Christ) expelled from their families and clans. Or the assistants, secretaries, and interpreters of the missionaries became Christians, and later pastors. The first Chinese pastors in history were paid about one-tenth to one-twentieth the salary of the missionary. Thus, both from traditional Chinese society and from the history of missions, the pastor has a very low place in society, and thus a low self-image. In Asia, it is often said that those who did not have the academic credentials to go to medical school or study engineering or business, would go to Bible college. Chinese families, with strong traditions in work ethic, hold full-time Christian service in low esteem. Training given to the pastor consists of lots of prayer, Bible reading, and hard work in evangelism. This "Bible school" tradition of pastoral training leaves the traditional Chinese pastor weak in three areas: liberal arts, English, and theological studies. It develops him or her well, however in other areas: living under difficult situations, prayer and dependence on God, and adaptation compromise while working under traditional-style, strong leaders. (One needs to add that this kind of Bible school training is being revised and modernized since the early 1970s in Asia, as Chinese church leaders, educated in the West, assume leadership of many Chinese Bible colleges and seminaries.)

In contrast, the contemporary young pastor has gone through four years of college and three years of seminary (often, more than that). He or she often does not realize that his or her model of the pastoral office is one of the modern, secular corporate executive. The pastor shepherds by leading the elders and deacons to adopt a common vision for the church. Then the pastor goes on to train the lay leaders and to manage the organization. Preaching and visitation are part of a complex web of functions. The key to effective ministry is the ability to articulate a clear philosophy of ministry for the local church.   The pastor's pay and benefits (including vacation, insurance, retirement, further study, and so forth) can all be negotiated on the conference table, both before beginning pastoral ministry, and annually thereafter. He or she is a social peer and equal to the elders and deacons of the church.   He or she is a fellow professional of the engineer, the doctor, and the accountants.

Traditional Chinese pastors are looked upon to maintain the values of the clan and the community. Thus he or she is expected to persevere under difficult situations (hence most pastors' spouses work to support the family). Often, he or she stays in a church for a long tenure.   The contemporary young pastor, however, has much less sense of loyalty and perseverance. The concept of commitment to one place is not common. Thus two-year or three-year terms for the pastor are becoming more common; certain American denominations report that their pastors stay an average of one-and-a-half years!

While lay people should treat (and pay) their pastors with respect, pastors also need to identify with the church and the local situation (the city, the town) over the long haul. The concept of loyalty needs to be reconsidered among young pastors. A balance of rights and privileges on the one hand, and duties and responsibilities on the other, need to be maintained.   And the different roles for the pastor — whether as a value-maintainer in the clan, or as a corporate executive and developer of the philosophy of the ministry — can all be re-evaluated in the light of Scripture and adapted for use.

Conclusion

The future promises to be difficult, complex and challenging. Every Chinese church is a multicultural community. People are going to come from all kinds of backgrounds and going to all kinds of destinations — single parents, abused spouses and children, divorcees, new immigrants, expatriate Chinese intellectuals, interracial marriages, suicidal teenagers, drug abusers, victims of litigation, young widows, and senior citizens. How do we face the myriad of needs and develop effective strategies for ministry?

We are all more Chinese than we think, including ABCs. We all are more Americanized than we realize, including new immigrants and OBCs. Perhaps the place to begin is to reflect upon the cultural complexities within each of us. Self-reflection can result in greater humility and a greater sense of appreciation of what God is doing in the lives of others in the Chinese community. We must not insist on secondary issues, but concentrate on primary ones — peaching the Word of God, winning the lost to Christ, nurturing the Body of Christ, and encouraging God's people to go into full-time ministry or develop a sense of purpose in life to make a difference for the Kingdom.

How we do things can change. Why we do these things should never change.

Opening Up The Future

The Chinese church in North America will face some uphill challenges in the coming century. "Urbanization and the Chinese Church," (Chapter Eleven) will update us on trends to be aware of in the coming years. The Chinese-American church will face tremendous transitions in the twenty-first century, and we need to move "Beyond the 'Chinese' Way of Doing Things" (Chapter Twelve) in order to be effective in such a changing world. We need to face some underlying theological issues outlined in this chapter. Finally, the Chinese-American Christian community will need to develop leaders whose calling is "Bridging Racial and Linguistic Gaps" (Chapter Thirteen), the transforming of society for Jesus Christ.

Urbanization and the Chinese Church

We have analyzed the Chinese church in North America from the perspectives of the history of Chinese culture, the bi-cultural nature of the Chinese community in North America, the history of the church and the history of revivals, and the current crisis in Chinese culture. In this chapter, I will attempt to look at the Chinese church from the perspective of urbanization, and identify ten key trends in the Chinese church. Implications and suggestions for ministry are also offered.

Urbanization from Whose Perspective?

There are many ways to look at the Chinese church in North America. One way is to see her as part of the urbanization process which is sweeping across the world. Urban ministry (or urban mission), however, means different things to different people. Let us see how "urban ministry" can be understood in different ways.

First, urbanization and urban ministry represent the response of the Anglo church in the United States, in the past twenty years, to the urban crisis in America. For many churches and Christians, urban ministry means ministering to the "inner city" poor. From this perspective, reaching the three million Chinese in the United States and Canada for Christ may or may not fit this pattern.

Second, urbanization refers to the fact that cities and their suburbs together represent a whole unit. For example, the population of New York City itself is seven million; but metropolitan New York, including suburbs in New York, New Jersey, and Connecticut, has well over seventeen million people. Thus the Chinese community (and Chinese churches) are "urban" in the sense that, while some churches are in "Chinatowns" and others in the suburbs, they all share in the metropolitan frame of reference. Put another way, Chinese churches in the city and in the suburbs share a common middle-class aspiration and set of values.

Third, urbanization should be looked at from the perspective of the global Chinese community in diaspora. If we look at the Chinese people worldwide, we find that the trends and lifestyles of cities like Taipei, Hong Kong, Singapore, and Beijing are shaping the development of the Chinese communities in Vancouver, Toronto, Los Angeles, San Francisco, and New York. "Urban" means "urban North American" together with influences from "urban Chinese Asia." The Chinese community is a global network of cities.

We shall seek to identify ten trends in this global urban network of Chinese people and see how these trends affect the Chinese church. Unfortunately, the Chinese church has been more often on the receiving end, rather than on the giving end of new trends; we are influenced by the world more than we are influencing the world. Understanding how we are influenced by the world, however, will help us wake up, stand up, and witness to the power of Jesus Christ. It is the first step to effective evangelism.

Trend One: Rich/Poor Gap

One of the characteristics of the contemporary city — whether it is New York or Hong Kong — is that the rich are very rich, and getting richer, and the poor are very poor, and getting poorer. In this context, the Chinese church exists very much as a middle-class church. We Chinese Christians have not been used to thinking of ourselves as part of the middle-class minority in the Chinese community. We have not been used to taking a hard look at the material and educational blessings God has given to us. Out of the one and a quarter billion Chinese in the world, how many Chinese have the blessings of receiving an education in the West? How many live in a truly free society? How many know Christ? How many have all three blessings?

If we recognize that we are in the blessed minority, we need to begin to ask: what is our place in God's purpose for the majority, beginning with the majority of the Chinese community? The majority of the Chinese community are the laboring masses.

Chinese churches and parachurch ministries are beginning to reach out to the workers in the factories, restaurants, and stores in the Chinese community in recent years. The Chinese church must do two things: get involved, and adapt her message so that the gospel includes good news for the poor, the oppressed, and the downtrodden. This will not be easy because we have been taught a different message in years past. But if we are true to the Lord, true to the gospel message, and true to people and their needs, we will work for change. Compassion dictates change.

Trend Two: Multicultralism vs. Ghetto-Mentality

A glaring reality in every major city in the world is the cultural diversity represented by city dwellers. New York City, for example, is the most culturally diverse city in the world. In one high school, John Bowne High School in Flushing, Queens, over one hundred countries are represented by the student body. What does this mean? It means that we must not only ask, "What does it mean to be a spiritual Chinese Christian and a spiritual Chinese church?" We must go on to ask, "What does it mean to be faithful to Christ in this diverse world in which we live?"

Chinese churches exist for a good reason. We exist to serve the immigrants who continue to pour into North America. But we must take the long-term perspective: our children and grandchildren will mingle in Western society, and some of them will, whether we are ready or not, intermarry with non-Chinese. Even now we are part of a multicultural society, and we do participate in the lives and problems of this society.

One concrete action Chinese churches can begin to do is to fellowship with non-Chinese churches and Christians. If we borrow facilities from a non-Chinese church, we need to seek a deeper understanding of their life and ministry. Perhaps we can adopt a sister church which is not Chinese. This is a first step we can take in learning what it means to be faithful to Christ in light of the multicultural character of heaven. (Recent short-term mission trips to Native American communities, and outreach to Southeast Asian communities in North America, are a very encouraging start.) This does not mean, of course, that every Chinese church must immediately become multilingual and multicultural. But it does mean that we must reach out to our neighbors.

Trend Three: Sophistication and Secularization

In the 1980s the mayor of New York City was trying to slow the trend of corporations moving their offices out of the city. His advertising campaign emphasized that in any given week, one is more likely to run into more "smart people" more often, if one works in the city. The city breathes life, creativity, and energy.

This is true. This is true of New York, Hong Kong, Tokyo, Taipei, or Amsterdam. If I were to give a definition of what sophisticated means, I would include these elements:

A culture very much defined by the upper middle-class. Although the term "Yuppie" was overused, and some have proclaimed that "Yuppiedom" died in the 1990s, it is still helpful to remember that the upper middle-class, the corporate and the artistic professionals, do set the trends in consumerism and behavior.

A culture is often defined by its "cultural wombs" which give birth to its symbols; in the United States, this means New York and Los Angeles. Small towns and villages are constantly bombarded by network news from New York and movies from Los Angeles. Three major New York newspapers are even distributed nationwide. We cannot avoid New York and Los Angeles; it is with us everywhere. Let us therefore seek to understand it, analyze it, and critique it from a biblical perspective.

The new is emphasized. We are under an impression, often an illusion, that everything is progressing toward something better, higher, newer, and more "sophisticated." The fact that our society is morally bankrupt is often hidden under the rug.

A sense of creativity and energy permeates the city. People move faster, think faster, drive at higher speeds, and demand better imaging in literature and media presentations. This can be positive for the gospel ministry if we know how to use this energy and make the gospel presentation attractive. It can also be misused.

A real sense of confidence and pride can often be felt when one runs across a New Yorker or a person from Toronto, Los Angeles, or Hong Kong. This can be good, but it can also be a facade. Underneath the confidence may be simply a broken life with no meaning, no direction, and no friends who understand.

A bias toward the secular, and against the orthodox Christian message, is often seen in decisions made in advertising, entertainment, education, and the law. We do live in a very secular, pagan world. Cities accentuate that secularity.

I would submit that these six characteristics — an upper middle-class taste, oozing from the city with energy and creativity, with a confidence, pride and a bent toward the new, and permeated with an anti-Christian secular stance — together comprise "sophistication" in the 1990s and beyond.

What does this mean for the Chinese church? It means we must understand it and learn to live in such a world as serpents and doves. We can live in a sophisticated world without being eaten up by its secular and pagan values, and continue to make a difference for Christ's sake. Sophisticated people are often broken people who desperately need Jesus Christ — and some hearts may even have been prepared by the Spirit to receive the Good News!

Trend Four: Time vs. Leisure

One characteristic of a smaller community is that people get up earlier, get off work earlier, and can start evening meetings earlier (some as early as 5:30 p.m.). In New York City, the average dinner time in the Chinese family is well past 8 p.m.. Some families eat at 9:30 p.m. We are under tremendous pressure to find time to do meaningful things. People are busy, they are tired, and they are stressed out.

What does it mean for the Chinese church? It means that we must understand this is the reality in which our Christian and non-Christian friends live. Instead of creating more pressure and stress for people, we must learn to understand their need for leisure, their need for time to meditate on God, time for family, and time

180

for rest and physical exercise. The church can adjust and provide for some of these needs.

Trend Five: The Collapse of Family and Sexual Ethics

The sexual revolution of the 1960s has made a permanent impact on American society, and families in Hong Kong, Taiwan, and mainland China are following that trend. Fathers are often absent from the home; extramarital affairs and divorce for the simple reason of "lack of fulfillment" are becoming more common. Sexual norms are disintegrating as we are bombarded with sex (of all kinds and perverted varieties!) in advertising, on TV, in music, and in every kind of entertainment. Young people who grow up with two parents at home and want to be virgins before marriage find themselves in the minority and under incredible pressure. They need our support, teaching, and encouragement! And when they do fall, they need our support, teaching and encouragement even more!

In both Christian and Chinese circles the topic of sexual ethics has traditionally been taboo. We are encouraged to find, however, that premarital counseling, and marriage and family workshops and books are beginning to be accepted and used by Chinese churches in North America. This is an absolute must, because if Satan can attack the family, he can bring down the witness of the whole Body of Christ.

Trend Six: Confusion of Gender Roles

Closely connected with the sexual revolution is the women's rights movement. One of the results of feminism is the confusion of the roles of men and women, both at home and at work. This spills over to the church.

Men are confused today on how to exercise their God-given "headship." God intends for husbands to lovingly lead their wives at home. This gives no excuse for dictatorship and oppression, not to speak of abuse. Husbands are to love their wives so much, like Christ, that they would be willing to die for them. But what does it mean to love one's wife when the wife is a medical doctor or executive making one hundred fifty thousand dollars a year, two to three times more than the husband? How should the husband and the wife share household and child-rearing responsibilities? And in the church, how can the spiritual gifts of men and women be optimally used without compromising what the Bible says about the headship of men?

The church in America exported women's issue abroad one hundred years ago, by sending women missionaries (both wives and single women) to China without defining their roles clearly. When these women went to China, they started preaching and training male pastors. So traditionally, the Chinese church has never had an issue with women preachers, until in the 1970s the Chinese church discovered that in the West, the woman's role in the church has become a controversial topic in the church.

It is time we face this issue and build models of ministry and family life that are both scriptural and compassionate, both faithful to the Bible, realistic, and relevant to our situation. It is high time we deploy women in the ministry of the church according to Scriptural norms.

Trend Seven: Low Self-Esteem

Part of the result of the breakdown of the family, and the confusion of the roles of men and women, is the lack of a healthy self-esteem on the part of city dwellers, including Chinese people. The whole idea of having a healthy self-image can be exaggerated, some have suggested. And contemporary psychology probably is more helpful in describing the problems a sinful person faces, than in prescribing answers. Nevertheless, we must recognize the facts: Chinese men and women often feel that they are not important. We often feel that the future is gloomy, we have no direction, and we serve no higher purpose.

Jesus Christ is our high priest and our constant friend. But we must present the love of Christ and the fatherly compassion of God in the context of a complete and comprehensive gospel. It is when we come to worship God and Jesus as our Lord that we truly appreciate the fact that he has accepted us as sinners, purely by grace. If I am accepted through Christ, I can be secure. I know I am loved. I can go on to die to self, live for God, and love others.

Traditionally Chinese and fundamentalists tend to devalue the worth of an individual. We do this unintentionally: in public speeches and sermons we often reprimand more than encourage. We critique more than appreciate. This is also true of our child training techniques. Chinese churches can do more serious thinking as to how to affirm members of the Body of Christ in a scriptural and loving way.

Trend Eight: Illiteracy and Technocratic Education

One of the important facts facing the American economy since the early 1980s is the utter failure of the American educational system. We train up high school graduates who cannot fill out employment application forms. A Chinese may respond: that is not true of Chinese high school graduates. I respond: not every Chinese high school graduate has succeeded academically. In some parts of the Chinese community, both the academic performance of high school students, and the expectations placed on them by their parents, are dropping.

We are witnessing an achievement-failure gap. Some are making it to prestigious colleges; others have fallen toward the bottom of the scale. In both cases, we are witnessing a widespread cultural and biblical illiteracy. We need to train our young people how to think deeply, broadly, strategically, critically, ethically, and biblically. We begin this process by first training ourselves, Chinese Christian adults, how to think biblically — deeply, broadly, strategically, critically, and ethically.

The task of Christian education in the church (including Bible studies, Sunday School, youth groups, family fellowships) should be more than "Christian" education in the traditional, narrow sense. In this day and age, the task of Christian education in the church should be *education* — teaching ourselves how to think, how to read, how to communicate. We have no other choice!

Trend Nine: Conflict and Law

Our cities are places filled with conflict, including racial conflict and legal battles. Chinese Christians need to learn how to deal with setbacks and challenges. Sometimes these challenges may come in the form of lawsuits, whether civil or criminal.

Jesus taught us to be both serpents and doves. Today more than ever, we need to learn how to be both. Traditionally we have been taught to love, to submit and to be patient. How does one live out the teachings and the example of Christ in the litigious city? Chinese churches need to begin an educational process in this arena.

Trend Ten: Secularly and Paganly Religious

One final characteristic of both Western and Asian cities must not escape us: every culture is religious at the core. People are never neutral to the God of the universe: we either worship him or we find idols to worship. The most secularized cities have their own gods. Witness the emergence of Satan worship, the New Age movement, and Paganism in the West, and the various forms of idol worship and spiritism in Asia.

The Chinese church needs to be more aware of spiritual battles that we are called to fight. The battle will become more fierce in the twenty-first century. It will touch more Christians and more aspects of our lives.

Whatever our convictions about certain controversial theological topics (for example, gifts of the Spirit), one thing is certain: the Devil is very busy today. Let us get busy, too, and take the offensive in the powerful name of Christ.

Beyond the "Chinese" Way
of Doing Things

Cultural Change: Some Theological Questions

One point is clear: it is no longer possible to say with confidence who is a "pure Chinese" or who is "totally American." Based on a person's date and place of birth, or the historical period of a person's immigration into North America, one can delineate different types of sub-cultural groups. Chinese culture is in the process of transformation; it has been in transformation since the mid-nineteenth century. In order to better minister to Chinese people today, we must wrestle with this reality of change. The reality of Chinese in places such as Indonesia and Singapore, who no longer identify with the Chinese-speaking community and churches, is very telling. Are we ready to cope with change? Does the Chinese church have a philosophy of ministry and evangelism which takes into account cultural change?

More importantly, are we ready to address this phenomenon of cultural change theologically? In recent years, evangelical Chinese leaders have begun to explore the whole field of "theology of culture." Men and women are trained in graduate schools of theology in the whole area of theology of culture. One result of this sensitivity to culture is that we find expressions of the Christian faith in various sub-cultures (for example, Hong Kong youth, American-born Chinese young adults, mainland Chinese in North America, and so forth). But I think it is necessary to define what we mean when we say that we need to address theologically the issue of cultural change.

When we speak of a "theology of culture," we often mean many things. For example, the theology of culture may refer to the biblical basis and justification for Christian involvement in the pursuit of art, science, education, economics, and social and political action. It is the search for a Christian perspective on these spheres of cultural endeavor. In traditional theology we call this effort the "cultural mandate."

Secondly, we make specific evaluations and critiques of contemporary (or historical) examples of art, whether it be works of literature, film, visual arts, or popular entertainment. Thus, book and film reviews are very much an important part of Christian reflection on the contemporary world.

Thirdly, "theology of culture" may refer to the discussion of the meaning of the process of cross-cultural evangelism and ministry. In this area, evangelicals, both Western and Chinese, have concentrated more on the "how" in cross-cultural evangelism, than in the "what" of cultural dynamics. We have been more interested in effectiveness than in a more refined understanding of what culture and cross-cultural works are all about. In this connection, the church has listened to the voices of the social and behavioral scientists without giving an adequate theological response. (Harvie Conn's *Eternal Word and Changing Worlds* was a groundbreaking attempt at this "trialogue" between theology, missions, and anthropology.)

Fourthly, the "theology of culture" brings us to the inquiry into the justification for, and the process of expressing and applying the gospel in a particular cultural context. This is the whole area of indigenization, or contextualization. We, the Chinese church, have talked a lot about the need for "contextual theology." What we have accomplished, however, are more indigenized forms of theological education. There has been little contextual theology done, partly because it requires a combination of skills in Bible, theology, Chinese history and literature, and the social sciences. Others have called for a "redemption of culture" and "Christian counter-culture."

Fifthly, the "theology of culture" may make inquiry into the whole process of cultural transformation. This is our concern here. We need to respond to the reality of cultural change, and make a proper theological response to anthropological insights concerning cultural change. Here we will raise several issues concerning the work of the Holy Spirit in history, that is, the superintending work of the Holy Spirit over the process of cultural change.

The first question we may ask is, how is God related to the process of history? We evangelicals have been critical of "process theology," which identifies God as part of the historical process of change. God becomes identified with his creation. Clark Pinnock, in *The Openness of God* (1995), would have us think of God as identifying with our surprises, so that our surprises are God's surprises! A Bible-based theology of cultural change would not do anything like this. However, the following question is worth asking: is our concept of God as a person so static that any concept of God as dynamic is ruled out? Consider how we teach the doctrine of God. We list God's attributes and then classify them as communicable or incommunicable. We speak of God as infinite over his creation: omnipresent, omniscient, omnipotent. God is often presented as a static person rather than as a Creator, a creative person and a Sovereign Lord whose mind is characterized by infinite variety and power.

God is working out his eternal decree at every moment in history. Granted, the essence of God does not change. Only his creation would change. But as we come to know God in the person of Jesus we learn of him growing from perfection to perfection (Luke 2:52; Hebrews 5:8). What does this mean for us? What does this say about the dynamic character of Jesus and of God? While on the one hand, God does not change and becomes something else other than himself; on the other hand, our description of his Godhood as a static being may need improvement.

The second question has to do with the Holy Spirit's work in redemption and in God's self-disclosure. When the Holy Spirit inspired humans to speak and write the Word of God, in what sense was he superintending the divine plan of revelation, and in what sense was he also addressing concrete human problems in a specific cultural context? (Scholars such as Charles Kraft would have us see that God, the communicator, addressed concrete human situations when he revealed himself.) Does the Holy Spirit do both? If so, is our doctrine of inspiration adequate to address both the "inspirational" and the "communicational" dimension of revelation?

This question makes some evangelicals uneasy. Let me add that God did come in the fullness of time to redeem his people, and to bring his self-revelation to a climax in the person of Jesus Christ, God the Son. God sovereignly chose to come in the first century. God sovereignly chose to covenant with Noah, Abraham, Isaac, Jacob, and the people of ancient Israel. In doing so, God's Word came to his people — in those specific time-space situations — and transformed the context. Yet at the same time, the context — with all its human agony, struggle and sin — makes the text all the more meaningful. Here, we need to do a lot more homework in studying the original cultural context in which the Bible was written, without giving up any conviction in God's sovereign work in inspiration.

A third set of questions relates to the human writers of Scripture and the original hearers (or readers) of Scripture. In what sense can we say that the original human writers of Scripture were not influenced by their culture when they wrote by divine inspiration? Or did the Holy Spirit so inspire them that he superintended over the whole process of culture, personality, and specific circumstances? What about the original hearers of revelation, for example, the people of Israel at Mount Sinai, or the crowd by the Sea of Galilee? Revelation, we have said, is both the self-disclosure of God (and his plan of redemption) and a divine address to human problems. And all human beings live in one cultural context or another.

We may ask: how many worldviews are there represented in the Bible? For example, in the book of Acts, how many cultures, or subcultures, can we identify as we see the gospel go forth from Jerusalem into Judea and Samaria, and into the ends of the world? The church in Jerusalem, for example, was probably all Jewish in culture (worldview), and the church in Antioch, perhaps 30% Greek, 70% Jewish. The churches in Asia Minor might have been 50% Greek, 50% Jewish. The churches in Macedonia and Greece might have been 70% Greek, 30% Jewish. It may not be possible to say therefore, that there are only "two cultures," Jewish and Greek. (What implication can we draw about our understanding of OBC/ABC distinctions and differences?) On top of this process of cultural change which accounts for the different gradations of Jewish/Hellenistic combinations, we may ask which is the New Testament's worldview? Does the New Testament itself provide another (third?) worldview? In what sense is God's revelation in the New Testament a worldview? In what sense is it different from the Jewish and Greek worldviews?

My friend Dr. Che-Bin Tan would suggest that while the New Testament does not provide a worldview (in the same sense as the Jewish and the Greek were worldviews), it does provide the basis for the transformation of all cultures and worldviews, whether Jewish, Greek, or otherwise. Perhaps I can put it another way: the kind of response which the gospel demands of us is so radical and deep-seated, that there needs to be an inner, deep-seated transformation of our worldview. This deep-level transformation of worldview allows us to make proper responses to the cultures in which we find ourselves, and to witness effectively to the biblical faith. This is transformation of culture on another level: the level of attitudes, values, beliefs, and lifestyles.

A fourth kind of question has to do with God's relationship to cultural change in general world history. God is never without a witness through the things which were made. His glory and power are made manifest. As a matter of fact, since the Fall (Genesis 3), cultural change and cultural diversity may be seen as the working out of the divine curse (Genesis 11) and human sin (Romans 5). We can classify at least three kinds of cultural change under divine judgment. First, there were the pagan cultures of biblical times. God told Abraham that the sins of the Amorites were not complete (Genesis 15); he hardened the heart of Pharaoh; he expelled the nations before Israel; he condemned idolatry and intermarriage with pagans. God is the judge of the nations.

Second, there is the secular culture of Western civilization. Here we have the indirect influence of Christianity through the centuries. We see the conflict of a human-centered cultural orientation (for example, the Renaissance) with a Bible-oriented culture (for example, the Reformation) . Through it all, we find it difficult, for example, to say whether America was founded on Christian, or deist principles. Yet God is in control.

Third, there is the case of China. As a nation, it is endowed with the general revelation of God (Romans 1:18-21). Yet the Chinese did not honor God, but built a sophisticated form of human-centered culture, Confucian-Taoism. This culture was humiliated before the Western powers. This same culture has been inherited by every Bible-believing Chinese Christian. And this culture awaits transformation with the gospel of Jesus Christ — a process which would take generations, perhaps centuries. (This makes the task of evangelizing the Chinese people both challenging and frustrating.) It is into such cultures that cross-cultural missionaries enter with the gospel and with the task of contextualization.

The task of expressing the Christian faith in a cultural context is never ending. There are two tendencies which the church must avoid: on the one hand, is the problem of *dead orthodoxy* — in so identifying her faith with the Bible, the church becomes inconsistent with the Bible so that her theology (orthodoxy) becomes irrelevant in the next generation, or in another culture. On the other hand, is the problem of *heresy* — in so identifying herself with the world, the church has lost her unique message and failed to make a biblical evaluation and critique of the cultures of the world. We suggest a third alternative, which would be serious about all of God's revelation — the whole counsel of God, nothing less — yet sensitive to the processes of intellectual and cultural change. To put it in another way, how far do we take the changeless, timeless character of the truths in the Bible? And how far do we take the "historical character" of revelation?

There are no easy answers. A hard, tedious task of exegesis and application awaits us — the task to which all communicators of the gospel are called.

Practical Suggestions

Do we abandon the bicultural model? By no means. Generalizations are tools — although only tools, nevertheless helpful tools. As we better understand the variety of subcultures of the Chinese community in North America we need to do more research into each subculture, or each "people group." How do they think? What are their values and beliefs? What things are important to them? How do they solve problems? My list of twenty kinds of Chinese is suggestive of the kinds of "people group studies" which need to be conducted.

As the church develops leadership to evangelize and serve the Chinese, she faces the acute need for multi-cultural and cross-cultural awareness on the part of those who will serve. Theological training and leadership training (whether in the setting of a seminary, an evening course, or a retreat) must help produce World Christians with a cross-cultural sensitivity. The Chinese church in North America is itself a cross-cultural context! To this end, training programs which provide exposure to Chinese or American culture (for example, North American seminary programs which provide a year in Asia for study and internship; internships for Chinese-speaking seminary students in American cultural settings) would be essential to the development of a whole generation of culturally aware church leaders in the twenty-first century. Long-held assumptions must be examined and evaluated; new philosophies of ministries need to be developed.

We need to learn how to live out the gospel in our contemporary world. In recent years I have been sensitized to the whole issue of women's roles in family, church, and society. The issue has been around for a number of years; it has such far-reaching implications to which Chinese evangelicals have not yet awakened from their dogmatic slumber. Beyond the issues of what women can or cannot do, there is the positive task of reconstruction — how to mobilize and channel women into positive constructive roles, relationships and tasks in the home, in church, and in society. It does no good to mourn the present or long for the return of the past. The issue is: what does it mean to live in our world now? This is the true significance of "women's issues." Husbands and wives are finding that their roles are becoming blurred. Wives with modern education and various talents and gifts are looking for meaningful ways of fulfilling themselves. This is bewildering and frustrating for the husband, the pastor and the church, not to mention the woman herself. Yet we are all in this together. We are all called upon to live out the gospel in our contemporary world. We are the generation who brought our parents over to North America for their retirement; who bought our own pension plans; and who will support our children through college. The task of living through the process of cultural transformation, in the industrial-information age, is simply "too much." It amounts to two to three full-time jobs! Yet this is what God has called each one of us to do — to follow Christ in our world, now.

The need for training materials for the church is never so great as now. Adult Sunday School and Bible study materials need to be developed, materials which would be sensitive to our time-held assumptions (along with their fallacies), faithful to the Bible's message and relevant to the very complicated world in which we live.

Meanwhile, we hold on to the divine revelation as truth, and struggle with the problems in the process. We learn to say, "Jesus is the answer." What are the questions? Are there any questions which do not have easy answers? And we continue in that struggle and in that process.

Bridging Racial and Linguistic Gaps

The world around us is changing at a pace so fast that we cannot keep up with it. For the first time in history, the human race can destroy itself with the touch of a button. For the first time we have artificial intelligence, robots doing work for us, and "cloning" threatening to reproduce the human being. Now we can choose to kill millions of unborn babies if we find them inconvenient to have, we can kill deformed newborn babies, and the elderly in Europe and North America are learning how to commit suicide before others do it for them. Meanwhile, hardworking Chinese people are caught up with the materialistic dream of making more money, finding a secure place for their family, owning their own businesses, sending their children to medical schools... and perhaps, if they have time, give God some lip-service of respect.

We, the Chinese, are caught up in a larger transformation process all over the Two-Thirds World: the process of westernization. "Chinese-ness" is changing. What does it mean to be Chinese, when China is importing Western high technology, when Hong Kong youth speak English as well as Chinese, when it is no longer legal to teach Chinese to our children in certain parts of the world, and when local-born Chinese (LBCs) around the world, although identifying with the Chinese race, have little or no knowledge of their ancestral language and culture? What does it mean to be Chinese?

From the perspective of the Western world, the Chinese people are among the many migrant peoples pouring into the cities of the West. In the twenty-first century, 80% of all people living on the face of this planet will be living in metropolitan areas. And in this "world of nations" — and I have lived in the City of Cities, New York — it is now acceptable to be an ethnic minority. (There is a real danger here: we Chinese evangelicals may exploit our American brothers and sisters' goodwill and turn it for a selfish end. On the other hand, American Christians need to re-examine their motives for doing "ethnic" or "urban" ministries. In certain circles, the remnants of imperialistic, triumphalist thinking still influence mission leaders. We need to strive for real partnership which is built on mutual love and respect.) The American missionary enterprise, for a century focused on overseas countries such as China, India, and the African continent, is beginning to look at the mission field which has come home to the ethnic minorities in North America. Chinese Christians are the "people of the hour." While still feeling the many racial and linguistic gaps — American vs. Chinese; OBC vs. ABC; Mandarin vs. Cantonese — we are told that there is tremendous opportunity for us. American mission executives look to us to fulfill the Great Commission around the world as cross-cultural missionaries. We are being recruited to join international mission teams. Meanwhile the Chinese church around the world is entering the "age of missions."

What does God's Word have to say about all of this? How should we live as World Christians? How do we bridge racial and linguistic gaps?

Before we talk about the "how," let us first talk about the "what": what do we believe, and what does the gospel have to say about racial and linguistic gaps?

Racial and Linguistic Gaps in the Bible

When God created Adam and Eve, he commanded them to multiply and fill the earth (Genesis 1:26-28). The children of Adam and Eve were to be one race with creative diversity. But Adam and Eve rebelled against God, and communication gaps between human beings entered the world in the form of a curse from God (Genesis 3:15-16). This rebellion and pride came to a climax when human beings united in disobeying God's mandate to multiply and fill the earth — humans built a tower which would lead to Heaven! God came to Babel to judge — he forced upon the human race the dispersion through the confusing of tongues. Imagine what it would be like had humans obeyed God! Would there be language gaps as we know them today? I wonder. When men and women rebelled further by all sorts of moral perversions, God sent the Flood and destroyed all — except Noah and his family. From Noah's seed came one line for the human race — yet there was diversity of nations and cultures. Unity and diversity were both intended by God in the beginning, but, because of sin, they both bore the marks of God's curse and judgment. That is the reality we find in the world after the Fall.

From among Noah's descendants, God promised a blessing for all nations (Genesis 12:1-3). And Abraham's descendants, growing into a great nation and occupying the promised land, would be a witness to God's power and mercy (Exodus 19:5-6) — God's own people in the midst of the nations. Israel was to be a witness for God, calling the nations to worship the living God (Psalm 100:1). Isaiah prophesied that the nations will come to Jerusalem and worship God (Isaiah 66:18-23).

This prophecy was fulfilled in the coming of Jesus Christ. He is our peace (Ephesians 2:20); he broke down the barrier between Jew and Gentile. He is also the last Adam — the head of a new human race, redeemed by the blood and indwelt by his Spirit. At

Pentecost the church — the visible sign of this new humanity — was given visible form. We now live in an age of the Spirit (Romans 8:9-10) — all who have Christ have the indwelling Holy Spirit, who is God's pledge to us for our heavenly inheritance. We await the day when we shall see and live in the heavenly Jerusalem, when every tongue and every nation will bring glory to God (Revelation 7:9-10; 21:24, 26).

Meanwhile, we await with eager expectation the revelation of God's people (Romans 8:18, 19), and while rejoicing in tribulation, we have as our ambition to please our Lord Jesus Christ. We are to begin with Jerusalem, and empowered with the Holy Spirit, proclaim the gospel unto the uttermost parts of the earth (Acts 1:8). When Christ's church shall gather around the throne in heaven, we shall see his people from every people and every nation — because God's people have fulfilled the Great Commission and have proclaimed the gospel as cross-cultural missionaries!

This is our vision: to let the earth hear God's voice. This is our mandate: to preach the gospel among all peoples — our own Chinese kin, and all non-Chinese as well. This is our motive: not to perpetuate the Chinese culture, not to embrace Western culture wholesale for its own sake, but to seek God's kingdom and his righteousness, and be renewed by the transformation of our mind as to what is acceptable, what is good, what is the will of God in both Chinese and non-Chinese cultures (Matthew 6:33; Romans 12:2).

How many are living according to this vision? How many are obeying the mandate? Who has honestly dealt with their motives in the church? What would Christ say to the Chinese church?

The Chinese Christian Experience of Racial and Linguistic Gaps

The Chinese church has largely followed the secular Chinese people in their concept of culture and crossing cultural barriers.

The Chinese layperson follows his or her secular counterpart; the Chinese church leader follows his or her laypeople...

Jesus says, "You are the salt of the earth." But we have reversed the whole thing: we have allowed the world to be the salt in our lives.

Traditionally, the Chinese people held a tremendous pride in their own culture. China was *tian xia*, the center of the cultured universe. All other peoples were regarded as barbarians. I wonder if we compare every nation and people in the world, how would the Chinese people rank in terms of ethnocentrism and pride? I dare to guess that we would be among the top ten... perhaps a medal winner? Paul tells us in Romans 1:18-21 that all humans know God, that we are without excuse. But in response to God's revelation, the Chinese people have constructed one of the highest forms of human-centered culture: a mixture of Confucianism, Taoism, and Buddhism. The result: isolation from other nations, and humiliation, defeat, and suffering for one hundred fifty years.

China's pride was wounded. A sense of superiority turned into a scramble for anything Western in order to restore China's strength and dignity.

Pride and wounded pride; superiority and inferiority — such a combination was painful. The Chinese people "ate bitterness" decade after decade. Wounded pride sought a restoration of national dignity.

Was pride restored? For the Communists, "the Chinese people stood up" on October 1, 1949. For overseas Chinese, modernization in Taiwan, a market economy in Hong Kong, and hardworking businessmen and women hoping for their children's success in Southeast Asia, Europe, and North America — all of this aimed at an unspoken goal: the restoration of pride. But the pride of the Chinese people today is highly pragmatic. Whatever works is right: one would employ any means in order to make more money, to earn another degree from the university, to open one's own retail business, to obtain immigrant/citizen status. In a relativistic world which is post-Christian, the Chinese participate eagerly in a "dog eat dog" race for survival, success, and prosperity. And wherever the immigrants went, they bore ethnic Chinese, a fact which each new migrant generation could not accept or deal with. Both parent and child (whether the first, second, third, or fourth generation) experience the malaise of rootlessness. Can pride be found for the rootless overseas Chinese?

In the midst of all this — the quest for China's restored pride, salvation, and dignity — the gospel was brought to China and the Chinese church grew up. Today there is a strong, vibrant church in mainland China, and thousands of congregations overseas. How do we face the racial and linguistic gaps? How do we imitate the biblical model of the heavenly Jerusalem? Where do we begin?

Bridging Racial and Linguistic Gaps

If one takes the gospel seriously and faces the plight of the Chinese people, one could see that the distance between the ideal and the real is too great. The task is too big. What can one person do? What can a small group of Christians do?

A Realistic Goal

We need to first ask ourselves what we are trying to accomplish. For some, our goal is to raise up cross-cultural missionaries among the Chinese of the diaspora. We want to encourage ABCs to go as cross-cultural missionaries, since they are more adaptable to different cultures. And as we look at the small number of cross-cultural missionaries sent from among Chinese Christians in North America, we find indeed that the majority of them are ABCs, or English-speaking Chinese. (This, of course, is not to exclude the need to mobilize OBCs to evangelize to the non-Chinese people; it only vividly demonstrates the need to mobilize OBCs.)

For some, our calling is to see the development of cross-cultural congregations. Church growth experts will tell us that people want to worship with people in their own culture. The inertia and resistance which accompany Chinese racial pride tells us the same thing. So what do we do? Try as hard as we can to build congregations in which Chinese and non-Chinese worship together? Yes, it would reflect the diversity of Christ's church in concrete terms, and ABCs and Asian-Americans are planting such churches. But how intimate can first generation immigrants get with non-Chinese people in the same congregation?

For others, the goal is to learn to cooperate with the Western missionary enterprise as partners. We need to be careful here not to exploit the generosity of our Western brothers and sisters, at a moment just when we Chinese (and other non-western peoples) are becoming leaders in the global Christian community. We need to cooperate, yes, but on terms of mutual respect and dignity. Let the Westerner get rid of his or her imperialistic attitudes. And let us Chinese get rid of a mentality of dependency and stand up to take care of our own needs! And let us Chinese learn to take of others' needs too, and participate in the worldwide missionary enterprise, as partners with our Western *and* Two-Thirds World brothers and sisters!

For still others, such as leaders in the CCCOWE movement, the goal should be a brotherly outreach to Chinese of different subcultures: mainland China, Taiwan, Hong Kong, local-born, Mandarin, Cantonese, Taiwanese, Shanghai, Foochow, Swatow, English, Spanish, Indonesian, Portuguese. If that is the goal, I would suggest that we concentrate on the key issue of developing pastors, leaders, and missionaries from among LBCs, and to bridge the OBC-LBC gap in the Chinese church in different parts of the world. As one of my superiors in church planting used to say: one can program only as much as one can staff. Leadership development is never as crucial as today. Today we have to face the question: leadership training in what language? English? Indonesian? Spanish? Are we ready for this?

Perhaps, after all is said and done, what all of us need to aim for is a truly biblical, *radical cross-cultural mindset*. This mentality seeks to be Christ's servants among all peoples, Chinese or non-Chinese. As Rev. Morley Lee says, "God so loves *the world* (John 3:16)!" Are we, Chinese evangelicals, willing to reach out in this way, pay the price, suffer the inconveniences, and do the work of ambassadors?

We need to know that our goal comes from knowing our calling from the Lord. As we seek to fulfill our calling, we need to face ourselves, our motives, our inadequacies, and our sense of insecurity.

A Spiritual Dynamic

To bridge the racial and linguistic gaps around us, we need to first be emptied. We will fill the void around us if we first create a void inside us. Jesus invites us to come to him and repent: "Blessed are the poor in spirit... blessed are they that mourn." Perhaps the place to start is an honest admission of our spiritual bankruptcy when it comes to cross-cultural servanthood. And we will let Christ make us need and hunger after his kingdom and righteousness (Matthew 5:3-6).

Christ will take our pride and turn it into a servant- and a kingdom-mentality. Only Christ can, and desires to, turn our wounded pride into peace and discipleship (Matthew 11:28, 29). Only Christ will take our raw materialistic pragmatism and turn it into kingdom thinking and kingdom living (Matthew 6: 33). The antidote to rootlessness is emptiness: empty ourselves in solitude, and there in silence and all alone, listen to the Spirit of God.

When we are willing to face our inadequacies and insecurities, God is gracious to transform. He will enable us to face our limitations; he will transform our meager capacities, and yes, he will yet use us, when we have admitted that he can bypass us and use someone else.

Dare we face ourselves, and face God? Christ invites us to come (Matthew 11:28); the hymn writer invites us to "turn your eyes upon Jesus." And there at the cross we will receive healing and renewal of strength.

A Philosophy of Ministry

We come to the cross to receive grace; we stand up and go into a world to serve. How do we serve?

The Chinese church needs to take seriously the multi-cultural reality which surrounds her. We must stop pretending that we can preserve Chinese culture. We need a truly multi-cultural and cross-cultural mentality as we pastor congregations, send out missionaries, plant churches, and engage in evangelism. One of the greatest deficiencies of the immigrant Chinese church in North America is the poverty of experience in dealing with a diversity of cultures. It is time we remedy this situation by creating experiences for our people.

Our goal must be the conversion of sinners and the growth of believers in the grace of our Lord Jesus Christ (2 Peter 3:17). Nothing else must compete with this primary purpose. If God has put us in the West, then let us reach out to our Western neighbors (including the host of Two-Thirds World fellow-immigrants living in the West). If God places us in Southeast Asia, let us reach out to our Southeast Asian neighbors. Dare we go beyond giving our money, and encourage ourselves and our children to live, serve, and evangelize among the "local people?"

205

We need to come to terms that people operate from their own cultures. We need to develop parallel ministries to serve each language and culture group. Then, God enables us to reach out and touch people in different cultures.

The Bridge

The bridge which we are called to be is *a bridge of servanthood*. Many OBCs and LBCs are gifted by the Spirit with gifts of teaching, leadership, and evangelism. They are also endowed with experiences in living in different cultures — Chinese-speaking and non-Chinese speaking. Increasingly, Chinese Christians are receiving some of the "best" education which this world has to offer. It is time to invest our lives in bridging racial and cultural gaps. The Body of Christ, and the watching world, need bridge people.

Christ came and lived among us; we likewise need to go and live among our neighbors — not just to exploit them with our Chinese worldly wisdom, but to serve them. We are called upon to be *the bridge of peace* — to serve as an ambassador of the gospel. Generation X is keenly aware of the need for reconciliation. May God raise up more peacemakers!

We need to interpret the gospel in a variety of cultural settings — OBC, LBC, and non-Chinese. This takes tremendous effort and energy. But it would be worth it. We are called upon to walk across the bridge as *heralds of the gospel*, bearers of good news. The good news of hope must be understood clearly, and then lived out boldly as we hope in tribulation, rejoice in sufferings, and count the cost as incomparable with the glory and riches which awaits us when we meet our Master!

There is so much need in the world today; who will offer hope, mercy, and grace?

Conclusion

In light of all that was discussed in this book, there is no all-encompassing methodology that will do justice to usher in the twenty-first century in the Chinese church in North America. There is no magic wand that will make everything perfect. There will be no new church system that will bring about a Chinese-American Christian "Utopia." What can and should be done is this: each individual must challenge himself or herself to become World (not worldly) Christians. Instead of conjuring up a new and revolutionary method of ministry, we need to become sensitive people, sensitive to the needs and questions of our time. That is not to say that it is an individualistic endeavor. It is a corporate mission in the sense that I need you to be sensitive and you need me to be sensitive. We need to become "Consciousness Three" people. This will be explained in Chapter Fourteen, "Four Roads to a Traffic Circle."

Four Roads to a Traffic Circle:
Toward Humanity and Dialogue

In this book we have traveled four different roads and have come to a traffic circle. First, we looked at "Chinese-ness" from the perspective of traditional Chinese history and culture, and saw a crisis of consciousness, as ethnocentrism was challenged by modernity and the international community (friendly or hostile). We have seen the erosion of the Confucian mystical worldview as well as the erosion of the Confucian pragmatic moral thrust. Today, Chinese intellectuals face the realities of anger and a painful memory as they choose between the struggle for hope or a senseless hedonism.

Then we traveled down a second road, and saw the overseas Chinese community in North America and Southeast Asia emerge from an isolated ghetto to a global, urban ethnic network of communities, prosperous and successful, but fully secularized as the rest of the industrial world has become. We have learned the art of "Anglo-Protestant" hard work, and made it into an idol. Traditional values, Confucian or Christian, are more a memory than a reality. Thus we arrive also at a crisis of consciousness — a culture with a void of values at its very core.

We traveled down a third road, and saw the collapse of Christian civilization in the West, and the struggle of the American evangelical movement to re-engage herself with contemporary culture and thought. The force which militates against this effort at re-engagement is an attitude which regards culture as evil and meaningless in light of the imminent return of Christ. The Chinese Christian community has inherited this anti-intellectual, anti-cultural and anti-societal stance from fundamentalist missionaries and Chinese evangelists. We need to re-establish a consciousness which is more engaging than retreating. Will we be able to retain the best of fundamentalism, with her commitment to the historic doctrines of the Bible, and yet be "in" the world as salt and light? This new consciousness remains to be developed.

We also traveled down a fourth road, and saw the crisis in the American church as the rural-oriented tradition is forced to face up to the urban global reality. We are facing each other: mainline and conservative, Chinese and non-Chinese, church, fellowship, and mission agency. Where are we as we stand in the traffic circle? We need to rebuild afresh our Chinese identity from the perspective of the gospel. And we need to do it boldly, for the needs are great.

From the Two Threats to Our Two Humanities

There are people, Chinese or non-Chinese, at what I call the level of Consciousness One. Consciousness One people are mostly unaware of the perplexities alluded to in our journey. They say, "It does not matter whether you are Chinese of American. We are all Christians." People in Consciousness One do not understand that they do not understand. Cross-cultural difficulties elude them. Whether they do not understand because they are fundamentalists, because they are ethnocentric Chinese, or because they are ethnocentric North Americans, does not seem to matter.

For Consciousness One people, the most threatening thing is to be disturbed in their comfortable ethnocentrism or dogmatic slumbers, because cultures which are different from them make them uncomfortable. These threaten their sense of security. As Americans are tempted to retreat from the world and enter an isolationist period, American Christians may want to remain in Consciousness One. Fortunately, many Christians today are traveling from Consciousness One to Consciousness Two. They are crossing cultural barriers by involvement in mission, such as teaching English in China, reaching PRCs in North America for Christ, or as a Chinese attending a non-Chinese church. They are involved in the difficult task of learning what it means to be a World Christian.

Consciousness Two people, therefore, know that they do not know everything there is to know about cultures, but they are learning. It is very tiring to live from day to day, being involved in cross-cultural evangelism. It is trying. However, an even greater challenge awaits Consciousness Two people. This is the realization that we have no more places to hide; we can no longer use cross-cultural evangelism as a shield to hide our real selves. We stand exposed in the global human/Christian community — our twin humanities, and we realize that we all stand in the traffic circle together.

Not all Consciousness Two people want to linger in the traffic circle. They journey on to Consciousness Three because they may have come to study or practice cross-cultural evangelism without having honestly faced themselves, baggage and all. But for those who are willing to take up the challenge, the journey to Consciousness Three, tiring and even more disturbing and threatening, is also rewarding. Consciousness Three is the level of living as global Christians. We are global Christians, who, by God's providence, have inherited one or more cultural traditions (Chinese, non-Chinese, Chinese-American, Christian, and so forth). We are able to communicate with others without using the post-colonial guilt/anger paradigm (even though this paradigm can mean good business, even in the Christian world), nor the colonial paradigm of condescension/subservience. We can learn what it means to serve together as partners, practicing servanthood, respecting equality and dignity in the Body of Christ, as the gospel spreads from six continents to six continents. We can relate to each other, individual to individual, organization to organization, congregation to congregation, board to board, movement to movement, as equal partners in the Body of Christ.

Why is the road to Consciousness Three so difficult? Because it requires that we be ruthlessly honest, yet at the same time be uncompromising in our love to Christ and to the Body of Christ. Not everyone is willing to pay this price. Yet we shall know the truth, and the truth — not only about the Lord, but about ourselves — shall set us free.

This kind of honesty has four components. First we must be true to Scripture as our absolute standard for defining what truth is. Scripture will challenge our assumptions, questions and conclusions as we look at (a) our traditions, (b) our contemporary context, and (c) ourselves. Second, we must pay the price and study hard to look at our traditions: Chinese, non-Chinese, Chinese American, Confucian, Buddhist, and Christian. We do so with a balance of celebration and critique, but always from the Scriptural point of view. Third, we need to be honest enough to look at our urban, global, post-colonial context, and the crying needs of humanity, whether physical, psychological, intellectual, or spiritual. This is honesty on fire, with a passion for people who need the Lord. Finally, we are honest enough to look at ourselves, our motives for ministry, our emotional baggage, and the scars we brought from our past, and turn them over to Jesus. We do this not in some secular, existential way as if truth lies in the moment of truth or the process of the search. Truth lies first and foremost in

Jesus Christ, not in our effort to reach out to him, no matter how honest and sincere our efforts may be, no matter how long the process takes. Thus we are honest to come to the cross, and at the same time we let Jesus scrutinize us in our honesty. We continue in our journey, always looking to Christ, loving our brothers and sisters, and letting the love of the cross shine into our hearts day by day.

Theological Reflections

As we look at what it means to be "Chinese," in other words, what it means to be a global Christian with gratitude to God for our culture, we are looking at the task of redefining ourselves and our beliefs. Let me suggest some directions in which we need to explore Scripture's truths.

First, our Christian faith must be ready for critique. This is the spirit of repentance, the willingness to grieve for and hate our sins, and to forsake them. There seems to be a spirit of remorse among twentieth century mainland Chinese intellectuals, as outstanding writers talk about the deep structure of Chinese culture, and critique the failure of traditional Chinese civilization to usher us into the modern world. This is encouraging, but this is not enough. We Christians need to be leaders in the spirit of true repentance.

Second, as we encounter both traditional Chinese thought (which dies hard in China) as well as the contemporary, urban context, we need to keep a sort of theological balance. This balance involves a sensitivity to the doctrine of the Fall, on the one hand, and the doctrine of humankind in the image of God, on the other. We need to see the discontinuities between the gospel and Chinese (or whatever) culture, and critique every culture in the light of the gospel. (Some contemporary Chinese evangelical thinkers are

213

reluctant to do this consistently.) We do this not in some sort of arrogant, simplistic (albeit pious) manner, as if all culture, being under the devil's dominion, has nothing of value in it. We balance this critique with a sensitivity to the truth that humans are made in the image of God; therefore the culture that humanity creates, even after the Fall, has valuable traits in it. We do not idolize a particular culture (Chinese or North American) so that our ability to critique it is numbed. (That is the error of Babel.) Nor can we afford to dismiss a culture completely, because there is continuity between the creation covenant and the redemptive covenant; there is continuity between Genesis 1 — 2, on the one hand, and Genesis 3 — 5 on the other. Adam's children in Cain's line are still made in the image of God; they are capable of building instruments and cities. Christ, of course, comes to build God's city on a hill — a hill called Calvary. He sends his people — those who have known him — back into the city to be the salt and light, to witness to his resurrection power.

Third, the content of our gospel message must include two crucial elements: the grace of God who accepts us, justifies us and welcomes us into his family, on the one hand; and on the other hand, the faithful covenant promises of God who establishes the relationship (that is, the covenant) between himself and ourselves — our relationship to God is the foundation of our relationship among ourselves. Just as Lesslie Newbigin talks about the gospel's power to bring humankind together, so China needs a "glue" to gather the 1.2 billion people together.

Did God make a covenant with the Chinese people? I think so. Acts 17 speaks of God calling every nation, every culture to seek him, and perhaps find him, because God is not far from us. If God gives the Chinese people the covenant of "common grace," we, the Chinese people, must learn to build a Chinese covenant — and those who have gained membership, by grace, into the redemptive covenant must participate actively and contribute our "glue" to piece our culture back together again — with grace and with faithfulness to God's covenant stipulations.

Fourth, the idea of the covenant also helps us to bridge the transcendence of God, eternity and time. For God who is eternal and infinite in his wisdom, love, and power, has decided out of his free will (that is, his sovereignty) to enter space and time to reveal himself as the Savior of humanity. Therefore covenant is God's entry point into space and time. Covenant promises are not necessary to God's being; it is an expression of his sovereign will. So God freely lays down his covenant promises in space and time — to Noah, Abraham, Moses, the people of Israel, through the prophets, and in these last days, to us through Jesus Christ his Son. Yet when God gives us his covenant promises, he binds himself to fulfill every one of them, for in Jesus Christ is God's "Yes" and "Amen." This is the mystery of the covenant — God is sovereign, yet gracious to keep every promise he has made. We, too, must respond by using our freedom (finite, fallen freedom) and come to Christ — we come to learn what it means to be beloved, and beloved promise-keepers, for God's sake and for China's sake.

What does this mean for our walk with Christ? It seems to me that the road to spirituality must include an element of satisfaction and deep contentment, resting in Christ and all that he is to us. There is much we can learn from our fundamentalist past; we must never compromise the quest for holiness, for though we are in the world, we are not of the world. But we must not become legalistic so that grace is lost in our attempt to be holy. There is also much we can learn from the contemporary programs of discipleship — books, tapes, and seminars abound everywhere — but we must remember never to treat the tools as ends. The end is life — life lived in wisdom and fear of the Lord.

There is also much we can learn from the mysteries of the faith, but we must never so extol mystery that it becomes esoteric, only available and understandable among the chosen, initiated few. The Spirit of Christ dwells in all of us who have Christ! So we learn, through the good times and the bad times, to rest in Christ and to be content that Jesus is everything to us. This rest and satisfaction does not lead to complacency; rather, it becomes the spring of dedicated, busy service for the Lord, because much needs to be done. Souls need to be saved; the wet clay pot, which is China, is falling apart, and we need to glue it back together. When we encounter Christ — our covenant mediator and the gracious redeemer — we are satisfied. We come to the Cross to be satisfied; we go into the world to be the glue and servants, especially servants in dialogue.

We do all of this gluing and serving realizing that Jesus may come back at any time. But if the Lord tarries one day, we are committed to staying on this earth for a long time, to work for evangelization; yes, but also for the maturity of the church. The road to global Christian consciousness, I conclude, is the road to mature churchhood. Come, Lord Jesus.

Afterword

The Onion: Receiving the Father's Gift

"For all have sinned and fall short of the glory of God, being justified as a gift by his grace through the redemption which is in Christ Jesus, whom God displayed publicly as a propitiation in his blood through faith" (Romans 3:23-25a).

There is good news for contemporary Chinese-Americans, and for all men and women living in this broken world. There is good news for Christians. That news is: we have a perfect and caring heavenly Father.

As Christians we have accepted Christ as our Savior. But as Christians, have we received God as our Father — one who has declared us righteous, and who has accepted us as his children? Have we?

The Spirit of Gifts

What is the gospel? It is the good news that Jesus Christ, by his death, paid for the punishment which our sins deserve. He took the punishment for us, so that a holy and righteous God, having poured out his wrath and judgment, removes his wrath toward us. That is "propitiation."

A loving God does not stop there. He does more. God brings home his salvation to our hearts by sending his Holy Spirit to us.

The Spirit moves our hearts and calls us with the gospel. When we are touched by the Spirit, we respond by turning away from our sins (repenting) and turning our lives over to his control (faith). When this happens, God the Father gives us three wonderful gifts:

1. As a holy and righteous judge, God declares that we are no longer guilty for our sins, but we are righteous. This is "justification."

2. God puts us in an intimate relationship with Jesus Christ. We are now "in Christ," and he is in us. The Bible uses words like "Immanuel" (God with us), "covenant" (God's commitment of love to us) and "union with Christ" to describe this close, intimate relationship.

3. God adopts us into his family, as his children. By the power of Jesus' resurrection (that is, by the power of the Holy Spirit), we begin to live the new life. Every day, every moment, is new.

This is the good news of the gospel (I Corinthians 1:9; John 3:38; Mark 1:14,15; Romans 3:23,25, 6:13; John 1:12,13). Every Christian, who has accepted Christ as his or her Savior and is living in close relationship with him, knows these precious truths. Yet I would suggest that, while all of us Christians have accepted Jesus as our Savior, many of us have never consciously accepted those three wonderful gifts God the Father has given us. This may be hard to believe, but it is true.

A person who has truly experienced God's grace and God's acceptance is a loving, gracious person. A person who knows that he or she is forgiven is a forgiving person ("Forgive us, as we forgive..."). A person who is secure in Jesus knows that he or she has nothing to prove, and therefore tries to prove nothing.

Yet not all is well in the church today. We see very little of that gracious, forgiving living. We see a lot of uptightness and insecurity; we see very few believers living as loved protected children of the Father. Could it be that we have never consciously received and experienced the Father's gift of justification? Could it be that justification, one of the cardinal doctrines of salvation which all Bible-believing Christians hold dear, is precisely one of the most neglected doctrines in our lives today?

Living on the "Yellow Skin" Level

Our lives are like an onion. On the outside, there is a yellow skin — elastic, tough, protective. We, too, have a yellow, tough, elastic skin. Inside that yellow skin, however, are layers of white, tender "onion rings." If we peel off the outer skin, we would see these inner layers, one after another until the last small layer is revealed.

Most of the time, we live our lives, as it were, on the level of the outward, yellow skin. We look beautiful, educated, respectable, middleclass, successful. We look OK. We certainly want others to think that we are OK (in Cantonese, *ho dim*). However deep inside we are not OK (in Cantonese, *mm dim*), and we know it. We say that we have accepted Christ, and God has accepted us as his children. But our behavior, and our inner feelings, attitudes and struggles belie that wonderful fact. We are not OK.

Now, God made us with a "yellow skin" for a purpose. Whether we are Chinese or not, we have defense mechanisms which protect us from assault. We need our defense mechanisms. But we cannot always live on the surface of the yellow skin. We cannot only live at that level. Our thoughts and feelings, our attitudes and our hang-ups lie much deeper than the yellow skin. For many of us, we will need to learn to peel that onion, and open up those white, tender layers of feelings inside. When we do so, we may not like what we see. But we will grow. We will live by the truth.

As we peel off the superficial, what will we see inside?

Stories from Our Childhood and Youth

Most of us grew up in Chinese homes, where traditional values were treasured and transmitted. Part of the great Chinese tradition is the emphasis on the family and on education. The sunny side of that tradition says, "Respect your parents. Study hard. Be a useful person in the family and in society." The shadowy side, however, says to the individual, "You are not worth anything except as a child to your parents, a subordinate to your seniors. You are not important, and you will never amount to anything." Many parents train up their children, more through chastisement and discouragement than by encouragement and praise. Many parents are used to saying, "You are useless!" One of the effects this can have on an individual growing up is that he or she begins to really believe that they are useless. They live with a lifelong sense of inadequacy and inferiority.

We heard many fairy tales when we were children. One of these fairy tales some of us heard was, "Daddy loves me. Mommy loves me. And Daddy loves Mommy." It sounds beautiful. And for some of us blessed, fortunate ones, we have experienced such a happy, lovefilled childhood. However for some (increasingly, many!) of us, this is only a fairy tale. It is like those "pop up" pictures which stand up when you open the storybook. They are only pictures propped up on cardboard.

Some of us have never experienced love from our father. Some of us never grew up with our fathers. Now I am not discussing here whether our fathers love us. There is a human instinct which every parent has — they love their children. What I am talking about here, is how a person feels on the receiving end. Some of us have never had the experience where our father puts his arms around us, and says: "Son/daughter, I believe in you. You will go far. You will be somebody great." Some of us do not know what that means, because we have never experienced it.

For those of us who have never experienced love from our earthly fathers, we encounter a difficulty (not insurmountable, but nevertheless a difficulty) when we accept Christ as our Savior. The difficulty is to really understand, appreciate, and to experience the love of God the Father. What does it mean that God the Father loves me, when I do not know what it means for my earthly father to love me? We sing about it, but God's love remains, on the gut level, an abstraction.

We grow up and become youths. We encounter failures. Perhaps the person we had a crush on never responded. We failed in a romantic relationship. We did not get into the school of our (or our parents') choice. We did not achieve in our careers according to our (or our parents') expectations. On top of some of these failures, we begin to experience tragedies in life. Our loved ones become sick. Some of them die. Other unexplainable things happen around us. And we begin to ask, "Why?" Before we know it, we begin to ask, "Why, God?" Failures and tragedies, too, have a way of becoming obstacles when it comes to receiving God's gift. They prevent us from fully experiencing God's acceptance, God's love and grace.

Substitutes for the Real Thing

So many of us — perhaps all of us — walk around with "baggage" on our backs. Some of the baggage we carry may be a deep sense of our worthlessness, a deep injury which we have never recovered from, and a sense that we will never succeed in anything again. Now as human beings created in the image of God, with truth, righteousness and holiness (Ephesians 4:24; Colossians 3:10), we do not really act on these beliefs consistently every moment of our lives. If we did, we would become insane. We do believe that we are, to some extent, OK. And we support these beliefs through substitute sources of true love and acceptance.

Many of us find a sense of self worth through our studies and our careers. And to ensure success, we find subjects and fields where we are more likely to succeed: accounting, computer science, the medical fields, and engineering. Applied science and technology are fields we are more likely to do well in — and less likely to have to come in constant interpersonal contact. So we prove to ourselves our worth and our status. We tell ourselves we are OK through our diplomas, our green cards and our mortgages. We buy a car, then a home, then find our spouses and have children. We think that all of these things will satisfy us and make us feel important. These things on the surface make us acceptable — to our parents who pushed us to success, to our American neighbors who recognize us for our success. Yet in these things we only find a substitute for the real thing. In the end, we have proven nothing.

Many of us come into the church with this sense of inadequacy and insecurity. So we do one of two things. We may stand in a corner. We hide under the carpet. We get lonely or depressed and then when people come to encourage us, we brush them aside. "I am in depression! Leave me alone!" Or we go to the other extreme. We become leaders. We even dedicate our lives and enter full-time ministry. Instead of hiding under the carpet, we now stand on top of the church's roof. And there we are tempted to control other people by our actions. Either by hiding under the carpet, or standing on the roof, we avoid coming into genuine contact with our brothers and sisters. For the lonely leader on the rooftop, one day he or she discovers that the leader next door is standing on a higher rooftop. They have a bigger church, a more glamorous, successful ministry. And that original sense of insecurity and inferiority comes back all over again. We have found, even in the ministry, a false sense of security. We have settled for the counterfeit of God's justification.

We try to prove something. But in the end we have proven nothing.

Counterfeit Marriage

Even in marriage we may have settled for the counterfeit rather than true love. Many of us get married not because we have thought through what marriage really means, but because we feel that we need to marry. The consequence is that we settle for a false love. Someone once illustrated the point this way. Two people are like two glasses of water. Each glass is only half full. When they love one another and get married, two glasses of water, each half full, are poured into one glass. Now the glass is full.

A beautiful picture, isn't it?

A beautiful picture. But not true love. Each of us, very often, is indeed a half-full glass of water. Half-full of true, genuine love for the other person. Love that commits us to seek the other person's good, no matter what the cost. We are half-full of that endurance, that commitment over the long haul, that "stick with it" power. Half-full of that gracious ability to accept another person's weaknesses, idiosyncrasies and unique traits. Half-full of gracious, reasoned responses to the other person's anger and frustrations. Half-full, in other words, of character. Half-full of maturity. Half-full of the stature of Christ (Ephesians 4:16). If we are honest enough about it, we are actually much less than half-full. Some of us are closer to the bottom of the glass.

And so when we find someone we "love" (that is, someone we find some attraction to), and we expect him/her to fill our half-empty glasses. We do more than expect. We actually, especially after marriage, demand that our spouses fill our void. What we are beginning to do is that we expect and demand our spouses to give us that kind of unconditional, perfect love, which our spouses have no ability to give us.

It is impossible that our spouses give that kind of love to us because only God can love us that way. We expect our loved ones to be God. While we respond to our loved ones only as a human being, a sinner does — with conditional, imperfect, very imperfect "love." No wonder we do not have harmonious marriages. No wonder marriages fall apart. Because we build our marriages on our sense of *need*, rather than on a prior commitment that, having been made complete with God's love, we now commit our lives to fill up the other person's life and ministry. It is as if my glass is already filled with water. And when two full glasses are poured together, they will spill over — the cup runneth over — or else, you need a larger cup. It becomes something larger, or something which spills over.

That's the picture, a beautiful picture.

That's true loving because we have first learned how to live as a loved one, in God's presence. So we give, we serve, we love. Yet many of us live our lives from day to day on a basis of need, not on the basis of grace, God's grace (Romans 5:2).

The Good News for Hurting People

The world is filled with people who have a sense of insecurity and inadequacy. The world is filled with people who walk around with a bag of inferiority complex on their backs. Now it takes secure people, people who are really secure, to help insecure people become secure. And true security comes from Jesus Christ. We have true security in the gospel.

The good news of the gospel is that, you do not have to have a perfect childhood, or have your teenage or adult years free from failures and tragedies, in order to experience God's love. Your marriage does not have to be perfect now, in order for you to know God's grace of acceptance. Because, if those things were prerequisites to becoming a Christian, then most of us would be left outside the gates of the kingdom! But my friends, the good news of the gospel is that God says, *he* wants to be the father to the orphans. He wants to be the protecting husband to the widow. He wants to be the perfect bridegroom to each one of us who would trust him and wait for him in love. And he is the one who says, "Come to me, all you who are weary and heavy laden. I will give you rest."

That is the gospel. The gospel is that as we come to the Cross, as we come to Christ with our baggage and our sins, Jesus takes over. We unload our baggage, and empty our bags at the Cross. As the song says, "Give them all, give them all to Jesus." What do we give over to Jesus? Our sins, which deserve eternal punishment. But we also give to Jesus our burdens, our failures and our heartaches. These may not be sins, but they certainly are the results of our sins, and the results of living in a sinful world.

God is gracious to us. He solves our sin problem. But God is also merciful. He solves the problems which result from our sin. He takes our baggage as we unload it at the Cross. And he says, I accept you. You belong to me. You are my child now. Go and live each day, each moment, altogether new (Philippians 3:9,10).

The good news includes the fact that you *can* be sure that God has accepted you (I John 5:13). While not all of us have assurance of our salvation (according to a survey I took a few years ago, up to one-third of the young people in a Chinese church did not have assurance of salvation!), all of us who truly trust Jesus as our Savior *can* have that assurance, if we take advantages of the paths of growth God has given us (worship, Scripture, prayer, church life). The goal of evangelism is not merely that a person makes a decision for Christ, but that the person knows for sure that he or she belongs to God. And the good news is that you and I can be sure.

Unloading Our Baggage

That is God's gift to us. As we unload our baggage. The problem is that it is not always easy to unload our baggage. Many of us prefer to hang on to our problems. What we need to learn is to receive God's gift of acceptance. The gift is: God has accepted us. The question is: Do I believe it? Will I accept it? Do I dare to live on that basis?

Receiving Jesus Christ as our Savior can be, for many of us, a simple step of faith. But receiving the gift of acceptance from God the Father, the gift which comes to us as a result of our trusting Christ, may be very difficult. It may involve a struggle. You may not be able to do it right away, by a simple prayer at the end of a sermon. It may mean for you a determination to begin that long process of struggle — and begin today. And it is a struggle.

I was brought up in a Christian environment. I have sung and heard hundreds of songs describing the grace of Jesus Christ. One such song I alluded to is, "Give them all, give them all to Jesus." I used to sing these songs mindlessly. But today as I sing "Give them all to Jesus," I often think of those brothers and sisters who, having struggled to receive God's grace, cannot sing "Give them all to Jesus" except with tears in their eyes. Not tears of sorrow, but tears of joy and gratitude that they have gone through the struggle. As we truly understand Christ and his grace, we truly understand ourselves. Ruth Chan, a Christian counselor who conducts indepth workshops on "Understanding Yourself," often describes her workshop as "a painful process." If we want to truly understand ourselves, and we cannot truly understand ourselves unless we also understand Christ, it will be a painful struggle.

The struggle, however, is worth it. It is very much worth it. Because ultimately it comes down to this: Would you rather live the truth or a lie? The truth is: God accepts the penitent sinner who comes to Jesus Christ. We say, we have justification by faith. Would you rather experience and live out that truth? Or would you rather continue to live a lie?

Will you unload your baggage at the Cross? For those who fail to do so, they will become their own burdens, and burdens for those around them. The church of Jesus Christ today is filled with people who, instead of serving others and helping others unload their baggage, are becoming burdens to brothers and sisters. They take up a tremendous amount of time and energy because they have not come to unload their baggage at the Cross. Someone once said, "If you are not part of the solution, you are part of the problem." The solution is truth, living on the basis of truth. Which would you rather be?

Struggling, Nursing, and Gardening

May I suggest a few things which may help if you choose to walk this journey of struggle? A fellow pastor and friend began to share with me some of the things he was doing. He told me he joined a discipleship group. Then as we talked some more, he told me that he was seeing a spiritual mentor to guide his walk with God. And finally he told me that he was seeing a counselor.

You may wonder, what kind of trouble did this pastor fall into, to require these measures? The truth is, this is not an out-of-the-ordinary person. He is just like you and me. And how much good it would do, if all of us were to do these things? And how can any of these things hurt us if we really want to grow?

1. A discipleship group: a place where you are accountable to another person or to a group of Christians, and where you provide mutual encouragement, healing and support.

2. A spiritual mentor: a person who would guide you in your prayer, meditation, journal keeping, reading, and so forth.

3. A counselor: one who helps you sort out your feelings, baggage from your past, and any obstacles you may have to love God with *all* your heart and soul.

A word about spiritual mentors. They may seem hard to find. But I think that God the Holy Spirit has given us many such people in the church. These mentors may not be super-giants when it comes to preaching, mass evangelism or administrative leadership. But inside they have that peace, stability and consistency which you know you lack. It does not hurt to walk up to that person, and ask him/her to share with you the secrets of his or her strength. "Would you teach me everything you know about prayer?" I know of another pastor who once walked up to one of the laypeople in his church, and asked that question. And that brother, having been trained in discipleship, proceeded to help that pastor, that fellow traveler in the Christian life, in the area of prayer.

As we receive help from our peers, mentors and counselors, we will begin to live out the life of the beloved, the bride of Jesus. We will be gracious and forgiving. We will deal with our past, and even learn to forgive those who have hurt us deeply. Those who have hurt us deeply may include our parents. As we come to terms with our past and our wounds, we learn to heal others. The church today is filled with veterans. These are veterans not of the war against Satan, but the war endorsed by Satan — civil war in the church. We have fought with our pastor or fellow leaders in the church. We have scars all over our bodies (that is, our soul) to show for it. What is needed today is a Veterans Administration Hospital, where all patients admitted are required to learn two things: 1. Nursing. The patient getting healed is also beginning to help newer patients recover from battle fatigue and from their wounds (Galatians 6:2). 2. Horticulture. Next door to the VA Hospital is a school of gardening, where veterans put down their arms and learn how to cultivate a garden, a haven of rest and hope which is the church of Jesus Christ (Matthew 11:2829).

As we learn how to make the church a garden rather than a battlefield, more people will be attracted to Jesus Christ. As we are transparent and expose our needs to Jesus and to our fellow strugglers, we will be an effective healer to the sin-sick souls who, by the thousands and millions, are crying out for a word of mercy and hope.

Many of us would rather not expose our needs and our weaknesses. Such hesitation is preventing us from living the full, abundant life which Jesus promised to us (John 10:10). The first step in the abundant life is the recognition of our need. We need to say, I have a need. Jesus put it this way: "Blessed are the poor in spirit (those who know their spiritual needs), for theirs is the kingdom of heaven" (Matthew 5:3).

May you and I be poor, so that we may all be richer (II Corinthians 8:9)! May we peel our onions, so that the Lord may make succulent, delicious onion rings out of our lives. He *has* accepted and loved us. Let us live as loved ones. Let us live the truth, so that we may give, heal and commit our lives to build Christ's kingdom among all peoples.

Contributors

Samuel Ling, president of China Horizon, is a bicultural churchman and analyst of cultural trends which affect the Chinese church. Born in Hong Kong, he has made the USA his home since the age of fourteen. Having been involved in church planting, seminary teaching, writing, and counseling candidates for the ministry, he is a pastor to intellectuals and a mentor to future leaders in the Chinese church. As a bicultural North American Chinese, he is a keen observer and hearty advocate of American-born Chinese and Asian-American ministries for the twenty-first century. He is a graduate of Westminster Theological Seminary (M.Div., Th.M.) and Temple University (Ph.D.), and an ordained minister in the Presbyterian Church in America. A lecturer in numerous seminaries, he and his wife Mildred have made Los Angeles their home since 1997.

Clarence Cheuk has a BA in philosophy from Wheaton University and is currently an account executive for a marketing firm in the web development and internet advertising in the Silicon Valley. He has plans for graduate school soon ... most likely law school.

Reverend Sam Chan is senior pastor of Richmond Hill Chinese Community Church in Richmond Hill, Ontario, Canada.

Reverend Alex Yeung, D. Min., is senior pastor of Mississauga Chinese Baptist Church in Mississauga, Ontario, Canada.